CHILD WATCHING

A Parent's Guide to Children's Body Language

SUSAN QUILLIAM

Photography by Jennie Woodcock

WARD LOCK

For Claudia, John, Madeleine, Paul, Philip and Stephanie

A WARD LOCK BOOK

First published in the UK 1994
by Ward Lock
Wellington House
125 Strand
LONDON
WC2R 0BB
www.cassell.co.uk

A Cassell Imprint

A British Library Cataloguing in Publication Data block for this book may
be obtained from the British Library

ISBN 0-7063-7330-8

AN EDDISON · SADD EDITION
Edited, designed and produced by
Eddison Sadd Editions Limited
St Chad's Court
146B King's Cross Road
London WC1X 9DH

Phototypeset in Garamond ITC Light by Servis Filmsetting Limited,
Manchester, England
Colour origination by Columbia Offset, Singapore
Printed in China

3 5 7 9 8 6 4
98

AUTHOR'S NOTE

If you have bought this book, there is almost certainly a child in your life.
You may not however be its parent, so I have had difficulty in resolving the
issue of whether to refer throughout the book to 'a child' or 'your child'. I
know that many readers will be parents, and my own experience shows
me that those who are not parents will often have a deep emotional link
with the children they know. So I have opted to refer to 'your' child and
hope that you can identify with this short cut. I have had equal difficulty
resolving the question of whether, when talking in general about a child, to
use the 'she' or 'he' pronoun. I am well aware that consistently referring to
one gender would not only raise political issues, but would be unfair to the
'other kind'. So although I have kept the accurate gender in real-life
examples, within the discursive text I have chosen to alternate pronouns in
successive sections of the book, to give a balanced feel.

Photograph on title page
For small children, the basics of body language are second
nature. Children are closer to that time in life when effective body
language, the essential tool for survival, is the only means
of expression available.

CONTENTS

INTRODUCTION

We spend a great deal of time teaching children the skills of language: how to speak, how to read, how to write. There is nothing wrong with that, for words are what make children fully human, give them power over their environment, allow them to develop ideas and reach their true potential. But emphasizing language can mean, all too often, that we do not pay enough attention to other methods of communication. We ignore, to our cost, the staggering ninety-seven per cent of personal interaction that is non-verbal. We rely only on the words, and then wonder why we sometimes misunderstand and miscommunicate. We even discount what our bodies are trying to say to us from the inside, and encourage children to do the same.

We do children no favours through all this. We cut them off from full communication with other people. We deny them the help we could give if we really understood, shared and enjoyed their body language. And we hold them back from true achievement because we never teach them how to be as effective non-verbally as they are with words.

I hope this book redresses the balance. It offers three things: firstly, a way of learning, step-by-step, to read between the lines of what children say; secondly, a method of communicating more fully with children through improving our own body language; thirdly, an approach to teaching children non-verbal effectiveness. These aims sound idealistic, but the book itself is nothing if not pragmatic. It will not be much use to you if you simply read it and enjoy the theories. It will be most useful if, from the start, you use it as a springboard to act: to approach children in a whole new way, to understand fascinating new things about them, to teach them wonderful new methods of dealing with the world.

What is Body Language?

A simple definition of body language is that it is everything except the words. A more complex answer would be that body language comprises the non-verbal elements of human communication, the ones that complement the verbal elements, accent them, contradict them, repeat them, regulate them, and sometimes substitute for them. Non-verbal language involves several elements: external signs, such as posture, gesture, movement, voice tone; the physical functions of our bodies, like heartbeat, breathing, blood pressure; the ways our bodies respond internally, such as butterflies in the tummy or tension in the back. These are ways that bodies interact with their owners and with other people.

Children know instinctively about body language. In many ways, they know much more about it than adults do because they are far closer to that time in their lives when body language was the only language available. A foetus experiences the world largely through non-verbal communication. A new-born baby relies for its survival on the body language that binds adults to it. Toddlers make body language their main way of relating to others. But, as they grow up and words take over, most children are

encouraged to forget, to ignore the ways in which they are influenced every day by other people's non-verbal communication, and the ways in which they make an impact every day through their own body-language skills. In this sense, our aim should not be to teach children about body language, but rather to help them remember it.

Body-language skill is essential to human success. Since the formal study of body language began in the early twentieth century, one of the most striking discoveries is just how powerfully and uncontrollably human beings respond to non-verbal communication. As adults, we can find ourselves undermining love by our eye contact, losing a job through our posture, alienating friends with our voice tone, without ever realizing why. Conversely, by being as aware of our non-verbal signals as we are of the words we choose to speak, we can radically improve our success in all these areas. This may be daunting, but it is true, and it is the reason why children need as much awareness of the principles of body language as they can get, from the moment they are born.

Body-language Myths

There are many misunderstandings about non-verbal communication; these need to be debunked and explained if this book is to do its job. There are four that chiefly concern me.

1. Body language tells it all. Of course not. Words are much more useful when you have to be precise, need to go into detail, or want to talk through problems, plans and solutions. But when you want to discover what your child's emotions really are, when you need to understand what her unconscious is trying to communicate, when you need to support your child fully and completely, then body language wins every time. In terms of understanding a child, it allows you to see behind the words; in terms of communicating, it short-circuits the words.

2. Body language is manipulative – you can use it to trick people. No you cannot. A child may not seem to notice your underhand use of body language, but she will not go along with it. Your motivation will show itself in your unconscious actions, and the child will receive not only the message you want her to get, but the manipulative message you are trying to hide.

3. In body language, a single gesture means a single thing. Untrue. Crossed arms, for example, may mean a closed mind, but they can also mean an anxious child, an angry adult or a cold room. Body language is not about interpreting just one element. Signals must be taken in context: the identity of the person using them, the situation, the other body-language signs happening at the time. Ignore these guidelines and you will constantly misinterpret the cues.

4. Body-language techniques work whether the person using them wants them to or not. Again, no. If you scream at an unwilling child to pull her shoulders back and her head up – because this book hints that doing so will give her confidence – she may obey you to the letter. She will then subtly drop her eyes and stick her tummy out, thus brilliantly undermining the strategy. On the other hand, no one is quicker to learn, utilize and elegantly develop effective non-verbal techniques than an enthusiastic five-year-old.

Happy faces and outstretched movements show the sheer energy and enjoyment these children feel. The adults, though, can watch for potential conflict or tears through body language. Shifts into sharp, hostile movements, withdrawn expressions or suddenly red or pale faces will signal trouble.

A vocabulary of body-language basics

Appearance shows health, gender, race, culture. Notice body shape, height, weight, hair colour and style, skin colour and texture, clothes. Gender shows through a range of cues.

Distance communicates relationship, status, attitude, mood, response. Notice position and movement towards/away from others. Their closeness shows a relaxed relationship, though the girl in front keeps her distance from the boys.

Posture reveals personality, emotion, attitude. Notice spine angle, muscle tension, limb position, head angle. Most of the children show excitement through posture, but the boy on the far right slumps, showing a low energy level.

Gesture shows emotions and importance. Notice body and limb movements, small gestures, head nods or shakes. The boy in the pink shirt shows through gesture how important the baby is.

Expression shows personality, mood, response. Notice facial muscles, mouth movements, smile depth, length and sincerity, eye movement, length of gaze, pupil dilation, blinking pattern. The broad grins of the hugging girls show their mood, and suggest extrovert personalities.

Touch used to control, support, emphasize, show emotion. Notice where and how a person touches and how he or she responds. Here, some children support by touch, others self-touch for comfort.

Physical functions communicate mood, activity, stress levels. Notice breathing patterns, heartrate, blood pressure, skin colour, adrenalin bursts, movement through stomach and intestines, sweat levels, body temperature, body fluids, body smell and taste.

Internal body language or what a child experiences inside. Notice mental pictures, mental sounds, skin, muscle and internal organ sensations. The slumped boy uses a head position typical of strong internal emotion.

Hidden messages of sound; words themselves aren't body language, the way they are expressed is. Notice volume, speed, tone, rhythm, pitch, stress. The hugging girls will talk in louder, higher voices than the boy in the light green shirt because of their gender and mood.

Conscious and unconscious actions: is a child doing something with awareness, like the blond boy swinging his arms? Or is an action unconscious, an uncontrollable response, like the nervous mouth movement of the girl with pink shoes?

When there is obvious anxiety – shown by the nervous hand-to-mouth gesture and the clinging arm – first gather information by looking, listening and asking if necessary. Get down to the child's level, moving closer to comfort. Only then start to suggest strategies for coping with the situation.

About the Book

This book is the result of a number of sources and inspirations. Its theoretical basis is the research done, mainly in Europe and the USA, on children's non-verbal communication. What gives the book real meaning for me, however, is the research on children's body language I have carried out myself over the past year. This involved sending out questionnaires to families and receiving their enthusiastic and helpful replies, which I have utilized throughout the book.

What I have learned through all this exploration has been laid out in the book in several presentation formats, each of which gives a particular slant on any one theme. The main text gives a core of information about a topic and how it can be used with children. The charts highlight some particular body-language signals. The panels focus on practical skills, such as how a child can build a specific non-verbal strategy. Finally, the pictures interpret the text and charts visually; they use real children and, with a few exceptions, show these children not in posed shots but in real-life situations.

Please bear in mind when reading this book that I am writing largely from the perspective of Western society. While the broad sweep of ideas I present is valid throughout the human race, cultural influences mean that, occasionally, specific elements of body language differ from tradition to tradition. I have pointed out these differences where I feel they are relevant, and look forward with interest to receiving further information from you, the reader, about other differences of which you are aware.

Using this Book

How can you use the different tools offered here to make body language useful? Here is an outline of the skills and strategies you need in order to get the most from this book.

1. Gather information. Cross-check what you read in the book with what you observe in your own child. Expect to find differences, for the general points I make are just that – generalizations. And expect to discover that you already know a lot about your child's non-verbal signs, as you are the expert. But

when, for example, your three-year-old is thinking, let the guidelines in the book alert you to the secret signals of thought that you have not yet noticed: eye movements, head angle, the shift in breathing. If the child can describe what he experiences inside, such as 'tingly in my tummy', this is useful information too.

2. Interpret. Does that grin mean your eleven-year-old is thinking, celebrating or plotting mischief? Look first at the context, place, time and situation; a grin during an exam will mean something different from a grin when receiving a birthday present. Next, look at all the signals to get a total picture; the messages may be mixed or contradictory. Finally, calibrate – compare what you see with any previous occasions when the child has behaved like that. What did he think and feel when he had that particular grin last time? Take all these elements into account before even beginning to interpret.

3. Be self-aware. Your own non-verbal signals are just as helpful a source of information as those of your child. Becoming aware of your own body language, external and internal, will not only help you fully understand what this book has to offer, it will

Body language isn't only about interpretation, but also about intervention. If your child offers a forceful physical statement, you need to give a controlled but equally definite response, non-verbally as well as in words. A firm 'no' or 'stop' needs strong body and hand movements to emphasize the point.

also help you check that you are setting your child a good body-language example. Most importantly, it will make you more aware of the effect your body language is having on the child. From the moment of birth, the body language your child experiences both influences and shapes him. Whether or not you are aware of it, every smile and frown you give affects your child, teaching him something new about the world.

4. Learn to talk your child's language. Once you have observed and interpreted your child's body language, you can also begin to utilize key elements of his non-verbal vocabulary. A child who uses a particular hand gesture when he is excited will feel appreciated if you notice that signal. He will feel particularly acknowledged if you use that gesture too, for then not only your words, but also your body language, are saying you understand.

5. Encourage skill-building. When you and your child are ready, talk directly about body-language skills. Western adults tend to discourage children from looking at other people, or noticing what their own bodies are saying. But by doing this, we block children's natural non-verbal ability. You can reverse the trend and teach your child to be aware of the body language he sees, hears and feels. Begin, if you like, with your own body language. Commenting that 'Daddy feels tense all down his back today' will not only give a child the vocabulary to talk about his own physiological communications; it will also teach him to notice, just from your posture, when he needs to treat you gently. Once you have started the ball rolling, you will find that your child probably notices more about body language than you do.

6. Introduce strategies. The ones I outline in the book can all be used quickly and directly with a child who is comfortable talking about body language. The only real limitation is that unwilling children will not learn from them. A younger child can be offered strategies as if they were games. An older child may give you a natural opening by mentioning a problem, allowing you to suggest a body-language solution. Talk through the strategy first, provide unpressured rehearsal with lots of rewarding smiles and hugs just for trying, then let the child experiment. Do not worry if success does not come first time. Achievement builds, and the day your thirteen-year-old comes home glowing because he used his 'confidence booster' before scoring a goal is a day that he – and you – will never forget.

A final warning. Body language is not magic. It will not turn problem children into angels overnight, nor will it turn problem parents into saints. But non-verbal skills do give you an extra dimension. They allow more understanding and communication and another way of looking at things. They help fulfil potential. And they are fun. If these benefits are what you want for yourself and for your child, then body language is what you need.

Individual children react to the same situation in very different ways; with anger shown in jutting mouth and arms akimbo, or with wariness, shown by nervous gesture and wrinkled brow. It is vital to interpret only when you know the child, the mood and the surrounding context.

CHAPTER ONE

READING YOUR CHILD'S MIND

Even your new baby, who has little to do but blissfully eat and sleep, drifts in and out of four distinct states of body and mind. These four states, in one way or another, mark the way we humans live our lives. They are, we might say, the most basic building blocks of existence. Your child's mind will experience these states as four distinct kinds of mental awareness. And your child's body will follow suit with four distinct modes of body language.

What are these states? Alert consciousness – often called 'uptime' – is when the child's body is happily and actively taking in, and responding to messages from the outside world. Using some or all of her five senses, or sensory 'channels', of sight, hearing, touch, smell and taste, she is, if you take the metaphor of a computer, inputting and processing data. So if nine-year-old Sarah is watching a bird, chatting to a friend, reading a book or enjoying the feeling of food in her tummy, then minute-to-minute she is learning about the world and interacting with it. The body language is obvious: she is looking, listening, feeling, speaking and doing.

Perhaps every few seconds for a moment or so, or perhaps every few hours for a minute or so, there has to be a pause. Reflective consciousness – often called 'downtime' – is when the child is stopping to think. She is, in the computer sense, processing the information she has been receiving, analyzing the effects of what she has been doing, maybe retrieving some bit of information to help her in what she does next. Sarah thinks about the bird, makes sense of what her friend is saying, analyzes what she reads, stores the memory of how the food felt in her tummy. When she does this, she needs to allow her brain time to work. Babies do this constantly and for quite long periods of time; in older children, the downtime needs are still regular, but shorter and more widely spaced. The body language here demonstrates a number of patterns that you can see every day, but they happen so quickly that both you and your child will usually be unaware of them. The most obvious sign is that the child will look away, perhaps just for a microsecond, using 'conjugatelateral eye movements' (CLEMs) – involuntary shifts of the eyes that allow her to process what is happening. She will look in one direction, to the right or left, approximately seventy-five per cent of the time. And she will do this from the moment she is born. From day one, you can, literally, watch your baby think.

The third state of consciousness occurs when, for some reason, the mind needs a deeper level of thought that requires the body to suspend many of its functions. This state of mind is sometimes called a 'trance', but that does not imply that it is a hypnosis-induced state, or in any way dangerous. Adults and children alike go into trance every day. It simply means that physical functions slow down and outside distractions may be totally ignored to allow the mind to absorb and react to what is happening at a level

Dorothy in uptime, interacting with Daddy, and in reflective downtime. Notice how head position and mouth movement alter from one state to another. In the lower picture notice that while Daddy is focusing on what he sees, Dorothy has defocused to switch off momentarily and interpret what is happening.

deeper than it does during downtime. Sarah, in this situation, may be peacefully watching television, day-dreaming, or being driven in Daddy's car. She may often be oblivious to what is going on around her, even though she is fully conscious, and able to react if called upon.

The fourth state is sleep. This complete physical relaxation allows children to integrate what has happened during the day; in the computer analogy, to store and save it in the brain's memory banks. When Sarah goes to bed, she has an immediate drop into deep, dreamless sleep, followed by a period of shallower sleep where she is close to waking. She will turn over, maybe toss and turn a bit, and drop into deeper sleep again. Then comes the first dream of the night, which usually lasts about twenty minutes, and is accompanied by slight body shifts and rapid eye movements (REMs). If we see sleep as a period of deep processing, then dreams may be the equivalent of mental filing and reviewing thoughts and ideas.

This possibility has some confirmation in the fact that babies, who have to integrate a whole new way of being, dream a great deal more than adults do. A new-born, for example, sleeps for nearly seventeen hours out of every twenty-four.

Balancing the States

Because uptime involves action, interaction, speaking and doing, we tend to think of this as the 'real', most important state of consciousness. And the temptation is to encourage a child out of any other state when we think she should be in uptime. So it is fine for a child to sleep at night, and for a new-born to sleep most of the day, but if your seven-month-old goes into downtime, deliberately turning or looking away, you

WHICH STATE OF CONSCIOUSNESS IS YOUR CHILD IN?

The four states of consciousness each have their accompanying non-verbal signs and obviously different physical states. Use this chart to spot the various states and signs.

	UPTIME	DOWNTIME	TRANCE	SLEEP
Example	Sarah talking happily to friends	Thinks about something a friend said	Watching television; day-dreaming	Asleep in bed
Posture	Varies: upright or flopped, according to how relaxed she is	A minute shift, tilting the head to 'listen to the thought'	Very relaxed	Slumped, prone, relaxed
Movement	Normal, whatever she is doing	A sudden halt; becomes much more still	Hardly any	Shifts position about once an hour
Eye patterns	Looks directly at whatever catches her attention	Looks away, uses CLEMs, blinks	Closed eyes, trembling eyelids, or defocused stare	Lids closed, eyes still, has REMs when dreaming
Speech	Normal speed, reacting to what has been said	May slow down or hesitate as the thought strikes	None, or slow and hesitant	Talks in sleep occasionally
Physical functions	Breathing and heartrate linked to what she is doing	Sudden intake of breath signals realization; breathing out deeply signals understanding	Slower pulse, blinking and breathing rate	All body processes slowed
What does she feel?	Unaware of internal feelings	Important thoughts may cause shift of tummy or bowel	Unaware, or heavy and relaxed	Unless dreaming, unaware of inner feelings

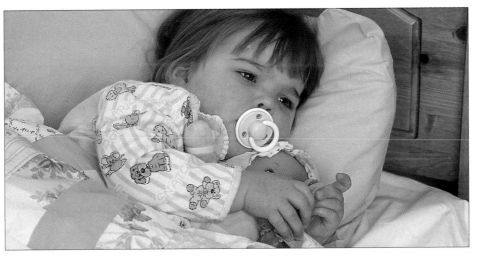

Three children in trance-like states – Dillon (top), watches television, Chloe (middle) falls asleep, and Victoria (bottom) recovers from hospital anaesthetic. What they have in common is the typical defocused gaze and slack, blanked-out facial expression that marks a state where processing and interpreting what is happening is the key mental task. Dillon is attempting to understand the programme, Chloe is reviewing and 'filing' what has happened during the day while Victoria's body is trying to make sense of the slightly upsetting experience she's just undergone. The differences in state are also noticeable through body language. Victoria's pale colour and sheen of perspiration show a child who is recoving from a physical trauma, Chloe's slight flush is her way of showing how tired she is, while Dillon's healthy colour is typical of a child allowing himself to quietly enjoy and learn from what he is seeing and hearing.

may move in closer, touch or speak, to stimulate her back into her normal, delightful, interacting self. And if your ten-year-old phases out in the middle of a conversation, you may feel irritated, thinking that the vacant look is a sign of 'nobody home'.

Downtime, trance and sleep are, however, the child's opportunity to process and integrate what is happening to her. So if you leap in and try to interrupt the process, you are doing more harm than good, and your child will show you this. The seven-month-old, forced out of her regular downtime breaks by your demands for attention, will go through a series of escalating cut-off movements, from protruding her tongue, hiccups and head shakes through to real crying. The ten-year-old asked to keep interacting instead of taking time to integrate may well get tetchy or simply shut down communication altogether.

What can you do? For a child who slips away momentarily into downtime, adopt what American researchers call the 'quiet' approach, simply giving the child sympathetic attention until she is ready to interact again. If you see a child taking downtime increasingly while you are interacting with her, try simplifying the content, slowing the speed or rhythm of the interaction or even increasing the distance between you so as not to bombard the child's senses with your presence. And when a child needs integration time at a deeper level – signalled by compulsive looking away or 'not hearing' – then provide low stimulus solitude, opportunity for trance through radio or television, or even a cat nap.

Sensory Channels

When your child is in uptime his body is constantly busy. Taking in information, giving out responses – and then taking in information about what effect those responses have – mean that all five sensory channels are working to experience what the world has to offer. The visual channel conducts what he sees, the auditory what he hears, the olfactory what he smells, the gustatory what he tastes, and the

---

CHANGING STATE

A child old enough to understand the difference may want to be able to switch at will from downtime to uptime. She may want to be in downtime for exam revision, for example, and in uptime when with friends. Here are some body-language strategies for changing state voluntarily.

To switch from downtime to uptime
- Raise head.
- Make eye contact with someone or look at something intently.
- Listen to what can be heard here and now.
- Breathe in through mouth in ten tiny intakes of breath.
- Breathe out through the mouth in ten tiny out-breaths.
- Repeat five times.

To switch from uptime to downtime
- Lower head.
- Look down to centre of body.
- Blink several times or shut eyes.
- Breathe in slowly through nose to a count of five heartbeats.
- Breathe out slowly through mouth to a count of five heartbeats.
- Repeat five times.

inaesthetic tells him about what he senses outside and inside, feeling pressure, warmth or movement, for example, both via his skin and in his internal organs. Many internal sensations are generated by thoughts and are often called feelings – when, for example, the thought of something threatening creates the stomach-churning we call fear.

A child's use of uptime develops from conception. A foetus, for whom the most important thing is physical contact with and survival through its mother, will experience mainly kinaesthetic and auditory input from its mother's body and its own. The enfolding of the womb, the body heat, the sound of the heartbeat – these are the important things. After birth, a baby naturally responds first to kinaesthetic and auditory input. He will need constant pressure and warmth, along with a regular, rhythmic movement reminiscent of the heartbeat, and a gentle voice. Within a short time, taste and smell become equally important, for they indicate food. Again, the baby's senses favour what it needs in order to survive: food,

warmth and an adult presence confirmed by touch.

As the child grows, priorities shift. Unlike many primates, humans are not dependent on smell and taste to track and find food, so these sensory channels become less and less favoured.

Kinaesthetic input is still important, to alert the child to pain or hunger and to communicate the brain's thoughts as emotions. But visual and auditory input slowly begin to dominate: sight is important because our world is full of things and people that need to be observed visually; and sound is favoured because our humanity depends on our ability to learn and use language. So the older your child, the more visual and auditory channels will prevail.

Children in different kinds of uptime. The girl in the pink dress is most interested in what she sees, pointing to draw attention, with wide-open eyes and mouth. On the left, wide eyes show that the dark-haired girl likes what she sees, but her tilted head shows that what she hears is also important.

Filters at Work

The body cannot experience everything. If it tries to, it goes into complete overdrive, and has to remain in constant downtime in order to cope. (This syndrome is known as autism.) Your child's body controls uptime input, constantly favouring what is important, either because it attracts, like food, or because it repels, like a scary sound. The body literally pays more attention to important events and responds to them more strongly. This behaviour often triggers a response, to which the child then pays even more attention, as nothing fascinates children more than

getting a response from their environment. Important things are, by this process, filtered in while unimportant things are filtered out.

Your child's body language shows you this filtering process at work on the outside. A tiny baby, for example, will use his body to signal, in a way that you cannot ignore, what is vital to him. He may, for example, thrust urgently towards the breast, or struggle away from a wet nappy. An older child will show many of the typical responses listed in the chart below. And the internal signs will be just as difficult for your child to ignore as the external signs are for you. His physical functions swing into action at the

WHAT IS IMPORTANT TO YOUR CHILD?	SEEING	
Your child uses body language to express what is liked and disliked. This chart describes positive and negative signs of attention to look out for. Notice, too, how often attention gets paid, how long for, and how strong the response is. The more frequent, longer and stronger the reaction, the more your child is affected.	LIKES IT: POSITIVE ATTENTION	DISLIKES IT: NEGATIVE ATTENTION
	Example	
	Peter, two, sees a toy	Sees a monster mask
	Posture	
	Sits up, head erect, chin up	Withdrawn
	Movement	
	Points at the toy, turns towards it, goes closer	Points, turns away, draws back
	Eye patterns	
	Eyes open wide, pupils dilate; looks at toy for a long time, then looks back many times	Eyes shut; looks away, looks down, refuses to look when asked
	Facial expression	
	Smile; brows raised, temporary forehead lines	Frown, or blank face
	Speech	
	Laughs	Whimpers or cries
	Skin	
	Colour may deepen	May get paler
	Heartrate and breathing	
	Quicken as he gets excited	Quicken when unhappy

The signs of classic positive attention are a wide smile, head bent towards the object and hands outstretched to touch it. His brows raise, his eyes widen to take in as much as possible.

first sight of what has caught his attention.

If all is safe, your child will then turn his attention to concentration. This may be so intense that he is unaware of anything else and his sensory channels are open only to what fascinates him. His physical functions settle into a relaxed 'maintenance' pattern with heartbeat, blood pressure and breathing easily providing just as much energy as he needs minute to minute. Four-year-old Paul is a typical example. Painting, he 'leaned the entire upper half of his body over the table . . . shoulders down . . . head bent . . . face relaxed . . . sucked bottom lip under top lip . . . eyes rolling from the paint to his work . . . intently . . .'.

Channel Choice

A child shows non-verbally what attracts his attention because he wants you to notice it too and to take action where necessary. It is the body's way of getting you to come up with the goods for the child's survival or development. With a new-born, you have to comply; if you do not, the baby will raise the strength of the signal to a level difficult to ignore. But even after acquiring language makes 'screaming the house down' an obsolete activity, your child's body will still want to signal what is important to him, so you can approve, support or rescue. Equally, you will want to

	HEARING		TOUCHING	
	LIKES IT: POSITIVE ATTENTION	DISLIKES IT: NEGATIVE ATTENTION	LIKES IT: POSITIVE ATTENTION	DISLIKES IT: NEGATIVE ATTENTION
Example				
	Hears a new kind of music	Startled by firework noises	Hugged by Mum	Hugged by unknown relative
Posture				
	Sits up, head erect	Withdrawn	'Opens' body: relaxes, lets limbs become soft; flattens against Mum	'Closes' body: becomes stiff and shrinks inwards; tenses against hug
Movement				
	Pulls head up from neck as if 'pricking up ears'; tilts jaw, helping him to hear better	Covers head or ears, shrinks head into shoulder, pushes jaw down to block sound	Moves and shifts to get more of the feeling	Becomes very still to reduce internal sensation
Eye patterns				
	Eyes may flick to one side following the direction of the sound	Eyes may flick to one side, then the other, as if to avoid the sound	Focus may drop or eyes may close to allow full concentration on the feeling	Eyes may fly wide open to signal alarm and discomfort
Facial expression				
	Smile	Frown, or blank face	Smile	Frown, or blank face
Speech				
	Is silent, to hear better, or laughs	Makes own sounds to block noise; cries for help	Laughs; voice pitch may drop	Whimpers for Mum; voice pitch rises
Skin				
	Colour may deepen	May get paler	May take on a healthy glow	May get paler
Heartrate and breathing				
	Synchronize with music	Speed up in panic	Slow down	Speed up in fear

Young children are usually interested in every aspect of something new. So what is important here? The fact that she is looking intently suggests that it could be the shape, colour or the way the light reflects off the ball. The fact that she is touching with both hands indicates that the texture of the ball is important, though the warmth or coolness may be interesting her too; if she starts to lift it, then she is probably testing out the weight. In a moment she may well attempt to shake the ball to see if it makes a noise.

focus on his concerns, to track what is holding your six-month-old's attention minute to minute, to be sure what is important in your twelve-year-old's life.

It is also useful to be aware of exactly how your child notices what is important – the specific sensory channel or channels he uses most. All humans have a hierarchy of senses. The choice for first place is usually between sight and sound. So when nine-year-olds Keith and Robbie go to the pantomime, Keith might come back talking slightly more about the colour and shape of the scenery and costumes. Robbie, on the other hand, may have a narrow preference for the songs and music. This does not mean that one will therefore become an artist and the other a musician; but each has a preferred channel, and that influences the way he experiences the world.

You can increase your child's general effectiveness by redressing any sensory imbalance he has. If your child consistently gets more excited by visual input, then make sure he has a high input of sound and music, and that he is getting enough touch. Sight may still be the most stimulating sense for him, but with greater input from other channels, he will become more knowledgeable about them. The effect will be a more open, interested and well-balanced child.

Information Retrieval

Once your child has received information from the outside world, she will naturally store it in her brain. But what happens when she begins to 'retrieve', to think again about that information? Research suggests that the child will use the same neurological pathways to think about things that have happened to her as she did to sense them when they actually happened. So when five-year-old Kim remembers her trip to the circus, neurons generate electro-chemical charges. These charges re-create for Kim a mental experience of the sights, sounds, smells, tastes and feelings that she had during the original experience – what a clown looked like, the sound of the drum roll, the sensation of the candy floss on her tongue, and the internal tummy wobbles she felt as she got excited.

Kim will think of these things selectively. Just as children choose what to pay attention to so they also choose what to remember from their vast data banks of stored information. And as well as remembering, Kim may also want to put her memories together in a new way; we call this

imagining or creating. Kim may imagine that the clown was wearing red rather than blue, or that the drum beat was slow rather than fast. As her mind performs these gyrations, and the neurological pathways leap into action, Kim herself knows what she is thinking about because a picture of a clown or the sound of circus music comes into her mind. You can get some indication of what she is thinking or imagining because her body shows signs on the outside. Psychologists currently disagree quite strongly about what these signs are and what they mean. One interesting theory, however, which ties in neatly with the proven fact of CLEMs (*see page 13*), has been put forward by Americans Richard Bandler and John Grinder. They suggest that each of the five sensory channels has a parallel 'thinking channel', and that each of these channels has a specific, recognizable, non-verbal pattern of behaviour. So if you cannot tell exactly what your child is thinking about, you can often – with quite astonishing accuracy – tell whether she is thinking about something she sees, hears, feels, smells or tastes.

The last two channels, of smelling and tasting, are comparatively under-developed in humans, so they will not be covered here in detail. Bandler and Grinder identify an extra thinking channel, which is that of a child's thinking in words. Once language is added to a child's awareness, not only can she read words and translate them into internal sounds, but she can also talk to herself in words, holding conversations inside her own head. This is a kind of 'internal dialogue', which she can use to comment on what is happening, debate possibilities, urge herself on, alert herself to impending problems. Bandler and Grinder call this essential element of what makes us human the 'digital' thinking channel.

Use the chart on page 22 firstly to learn to calibrate which channel your child is using as she thinks, but beware: each separate thought may take less than a fraction of a second. When your child goes through a complex thought sequence – such as remembering her teacher (visual recall) telling a story (auditory recall) about a soft cuddly bear (visual and kinaesthetic recall) and then internally commenting on how pleasing the story was (digital recall) – there can be dozens of momentary micro-cues that are over before you have even begun to detect them.

Taken in context, though, along with your child's whole body statement, you will probably be able to understand a great deal, even from the few cues you consciously notice. Twelve-year-old Cathy, when

A child daydreaming is halfway between downtime and trance, engaging in vital life-rehearsal. You may see feet tapping as she imagines walking, tiny throat movements for imagined conversation and tiny eye movements as she imagines seeing things. So if she daydreams, don't interrupt. Child at work!

asked what happened at school today, looked sideways (auditory recall) and then down (kinaesthetic recall) and accompanied those glances by a rather upset expression. If you were with Cathy you might not know exactly what happened, but you could guess. Asking 'Did somebody say something nasty to you?' would be somewhere near the mark.

Another reason to be aware of thinking channels is that, as with the senses, children find some thinking channels more important than others. This can vary from context to context. A child may think in a highly visual way when walking around a room full of pictures, but be lost in kinaesthetic downtime when remembering a bouncy castle. Thinking-channel importance may also have a long-term effect: a child

THE FOUR THINKING CHANNELS

You can tell which 'thinking channel' your child is in by observing the finer details of her body language. In this chart, some of the body-language 'micro-patterns' of the four main thinking channels are listed. Be aware that eye movements can vary from child to child, so it helps to calibrate your child's patterns by observing her when thinking and then if possible, getting her to tell you what she was thinking about – picture, sound, feeling or words. Here we take photographic examples of four children engaging either their visual, auditory, kinaesthetic or digital thinking channels. If your child is left-handed, read 'left' when the chart indicates 'right' and vice versa.

	VISUAL	AUDITORY	KINAESTHETIC	DIGITAL
When does the child use this channel?	When thinking of something seen	When thinking of something heard	When thinking of something felt or feeling an emotion	When 'thinking' in words; talking to self
Example	Remembering or imagining the tree house	Remembering or imagining bird-song	Remembering the hardness of the tree house, feeling excited	Telling herself what a good time she had
What movements or gestures might you see?	Sits up; holds head upright as if seeing; hand moves to eyes	Rhythmic movements; hand to ear; arms across body	Leaning in and down; rounded shoulders; gesture to tummy	Minute lip or throat movements; hand to mouth
What expression?	Brow raised; has forehead lines	Head tilted to one side as if listening	Face tilts down; expression shifts as emotions change	Head leaning to one side, resting on hand
What might her eyes do?	Move up and to her left (remembered image); move right (imagined image); or defocus	Move across and to her left (remembered sound); or right (imagined sound)	Move down, to her right (with some children, left)	Move down, to her left (with some children, to the right)
What about breathing?	May be higher in chest, more shallow	May be even, filling the whole chest area	May be deep; low – from the stomach area	High in the chest
How does she speak?	More quickly to reflect the speed at which images change, and more high-pitched	Clearly and maybe with the rhythm of the music	Often lower and slower; softer volume	Clipped and crisp, or overlaid with the emotion of what she is saying to herself
What does she say?	Visual words, about size, shape, colour	Words about speed, rhythm, pitch	Words about touch, taste, smell, emotions	Commentary words: judgements on events rather than description

who thinks about the world mostly in the auditory thinking channel may be a sounds-aware child, but may also become a child who is unaware and unappreciative of sights and feelings. A child may even have difficulty in using one particular channel at all; some children, for example, find it almost impossible to create a vivid image in their minds.

In our society, however, children need ability in all three thinking channels: visual, auditory and digital (Western learning styles tend to deprioritize the kinaesthetic channel). As with the sensory channels, then, if you spot that your child is specializing into just one, it is beneficial to lead her into thinking in other ways. If her preferred thinking channel is auditory, then give extra practice in visual thinking. Spend more time with her looking at graphs, exploring pictures, tracing or colouring-in the shapes of words. Try talking about them as you go, to 'bridge the gap' between what she knows about (sounds) and what she knows less about (pictures). Try to phrase your questions to her in terms of visual elements: 'What colour . . . what shape . . . what did you see . . ?' In the short-term, such concentration on one element may feel strange. Long-term, it will encourage brain and body into a wider range of thinking modes.

Using the Right Channel

Your child's preference of channel – both sensory and thinking – affects how you communicate with your child. If you spot, for instance, that, at a particular moment, your child is using her visual thinking channel and is deeply lost in what she is internally seeing, then do not necessarily expect her to hear you if you speak. Or if, in general, your child puts most importance on tonal qualities, either when she hears them or when she 'plays them back' in her mind, then make sure your voice as well as your expression tells her what you want her to know.

One exception to this, incidentally, is when a child is feeling emotional. Her kinaesthetic channels are then usually the most engaged and whatever her most natural channel, she will almost always respond to touch (*see Chapter three*).

It is also important to be aware of your own main channels. If you get enthusiastic about something, do you (usually) respond most strongly to the sight, the sound or the feeling? If you remember something, do you (mostly) see a picture of it or hear the words? If your pattern is, in general, different from that of your child, you may literally not be speaking the same

LOOK AT ME WHEN I AM TALKING TO YOU

If your child thinks in a different way from the way you do, it can cause problems. Adults and children whose favoured sensory and thinking channels are visual often need to look at people when they are listening to them, and they sometimes feel they are being listened to only when they are being looked at. Adults and children who favour auditory or digital channels often need to look away from people when they are listening in order to concentrate on what is being said, and they can feel uncomfortable if forced to make eye contact. It is quite a double bind. If your child thinks 'visual' and you think 'auditory', do not be put off by his staring at you. Reassure him that you are listening even if you are not looking. If it is the other way round, remember he is listening even if he looks away. Try watching his mouth when he is speaking rather than making him uncomfortable by forcing him to keep eye contact.

---

language. So when explaining things or asking questions, try using the sensory and thinking channels your child uses, rather than your own. Do your best to 'step into her shoes', seeing, hearing or feeling the importance of what she is paying attention to. Shift to her posture, gesture, facial expressions, breathing patterns or typical words, matching her behaviour. All this will not only stop the child being confused by your use of a different set of cues, it will also reassure her on the deepest possible level that you are receiving the message her body language is giving. And it will help you to communicate.

Lisa, aged ten, could never remember instructions she had been given. Her Dad, whose preferred thinking channel was auditory, kept asking 'What did I say to you about that?' As he did so, he also unconsciously tilted his head to one side. Then he noticed that Lisa kept looking up when recalling, and he tried copying the direction of her gaze, and talking in visual terms: 'You remember . . . we were standing in the kitchen, and I pointed to the fridge, and . . .'. Given a bridge from one channel to another, the chance to remember first in the way that was most natural to her, Lisa's memory for the event suddenly improved. Once she had remembered what things looked like, and viewed the memory from that perspective, she found it much easier to recall what she had heard.

Gesture Talk

Posture, eye movement and breathing patterns go a long way towards telling you in which channels your child thinks. To find out how he specifically organizes his thoughts, however, you need also to look at movement and gesture. Even a very small baby will put his hand out, upwards, with palm open to show you that he wants to interact, or will clench his fist to show that he is distressed. Many respondents to my questionnaire mentioned their children's gestures. 'Daniel's hands seem to move all over the place.' 'My four-year-old uses her hands such a lot to help her express what she is trying to say.'

How does your child use movement and gesture as thought-signals, and what do they mean? The first category is what anthropologists call 'emblem signs'. These mimic an action, and are used quite consciously in place of speech. Your child will pick these up at about the time he acquires speech, then there is a sudden burst in use and understanding between the ages of three and four-and-a-half. Yes, no, quietly, goodbye, one, two, I will not listen, I will not do it – all these are simply and effectively communicated by movement and gesture. Even without words you can understand what a child is thinking if he uses such movements, as he can understand when you do.

The second kind of thought-gesture is 'mime'. This expresses a more complicated type of thought. When your child is acting out something that really happened, the way he moves his body can give you valuable information about how he experienced it. Three-year-old Richard said 'The train went away,' then turned to point behind him, moved rhythmically, and ran on the spot. This told his parents that the train moved past Richard from in front of him to behind, that it went fast and that the sound or action of the train was rhythmic. Richard acted out with his body what he saw, heard and felt, reproducing the input as he experienced and stored it in his mind. In fact, until a child is fluent verbally, he may well give you more information through his movements than he can through words about elements of an event that you may not even have guessed he noticed.

A third grouping of movements and gestures reflect not your child's actual experience of what happened but his more abstract understanding of it. These 'metaphoric' gestures do not usually appear until the child is about nine, and fascinatingly, were not present at all in Western cultures until after the Renaissance when more analytical ways of thinking began to replace more literal ones. They show you how a child represents and organizes ideas and concepts in his mind as sights, sounds, feelings and words. If, for example, an idea takes the form of a picture in a child's mind, then he will typically draw out the shape of that picture. Ian, aged ten, sketched a rough circle in the air when talking about his family. This did not show that all his family members were

A child's gestures may not always be realistic. This doesn't mean the child is lying. By exaggerating, he is not suggesting that an object is bigger than it actually is, but is telling you about its meaning to him. Important things, or ones that carry a lot of emotion, are gestured as bigger.

A POCKET GUIDE TO MIND-READING

- Your child's eye and head movements reveal what thinking channel she is using.
- Movements and gestures show the detail and organization of what she is thinking.
- Her eyes, eyebrows, mouth and hand shapes show the emotions she is feeling.

---

tubby, but that he thought of them as a cohesive whole. If the child holds an idea in his mind as a sound or movement, then he may use a rhythm to emphasize further what he is talking about; John, aged twelve, always tapped one foot when talking about his favourite computer game. If an idea is associated with a feeling, then a touch gesture may be used; many small children hug themselves when they talk about 'love', for example.

Ideas can be represented in children's minds across many channels, so children express them in gestures that mix images, rhythms and feelings. When Kieran talked about running in a race the next day, his hands moved across his body to the left in a series of small jumps, rhythmically building the movement until eventually he formed two fists and made a sharp downward gesture as he described how he hoped to win. What did that mean? The direction in which the gestures went almost certainly reflected the way in which Kieran internally imagined the direction of the race, 'seeing' it as if he were viewing it run from left to right. The sharp downward movements reflected the very strong internal feeling he had when he imagined winning – a burst of victorious energy. And all the rhythmic elements of what Kieran did probably parallel not only his running, but also the way he talks to himself when he is urging himself on to success.

Making it Clear

Once you have learned to interpret your child's movements, you can also communicate more effectively with the child. Take a boy who, when talking about tasks that have to be done, 'marks out' those tasks vertically in the air, one under the other. He is demonstrating how he sees his pile of jobs mentally – in a vertical list with each one in a clear place and priority. If you feed back those movements when speaking you will be talking his body language and will be more easily understood. On the other hand,

BODY-LANGUAGE 'PUNCTUATION'

When we speak we use a whole series of body-language movements. These signal thought divisions and emphasis in the same way as punctuation marks do in written language. Children copy the movements as they grow, but the basics are there at birth: at eight days old, babies in a Boston University research study moved their bodies in perfect rhythm to spoken words they heard in languages as far removed as Chinese and Italian. Fascinatingly though, the babies only did this as long as the words made sense; if the researchers started talking gibberish and not a bona fide language, the new-borns looked confused and stopped moving. This chart shows some typical 'punctuation movements', along with their written equivalents.

WHAT THE CHILD SAYS	TYPICAL 'PUNCTUATION' MOVEMENTS
A specially stressed word, eg 'Mummy', 'lovely'	Blink at start or end
Emotionally important group of words, eg 'I want that'	A head jerk; eye or hand movements; a shift from one foot to the other
Adjective, describing word, eg 'big', 'red', 'soft'	Widening of eyelids
Beginning of important sentence	Small shift in position
Sentence pause, where comma might be if written	Lean forward or back
The end of a sentence	Combined movement of hand and head
Question	Jerk of the head; raising the eyebrows
Exclamation	Sharp movement of hand
End of thought, paragraph break if written	Large change in position, shifting legs and body
End of topic, different subject mentioned	Toss or turn of head
End of child's turn to speak	Sweeping hand gesture; a turn to person who speaks next

CREATING CREATIVITY

A baby's naturally spontaneous movements and explorations cannot be anything but creative. Later, a child learns mental restrictions that block his creativity and his body language becomes less creative too. Here are some strategies for recognizing when your child is being creative and for helping when he is not.

● To recognize the non-verbal signs of your child's creative state, look for: relaxed, open movements; serious expression with good skin colour; tiny sounds as he gives a positive running commentary in his head; eye movements to his right that signal imagined images and sounds.
● Compare the above signs with the body language of blocked creativity: a stiffer posture; smaller, more tentative movements; unhappy or critical internal talk; downward eye movements.
● To help neutralize the negativity he is feeling inside and to encourage him to experiment, use a positive expression, gaze, voice tone and touch. If willing, he can consciously take on the body language of creativity, relaxing with deep breaths, using wide movements, looking to his right to 'find' a new idea.

take a boy who, when discussing tasks, moves his hands slowly and vaguely in the air, with a worried frown. His gestures (taken in the context of his other body language) show that things are disturbingly mixed up in his head. Begin by acknowledging his viewpoint with words – 'Let's see if we can get sorted out,' – and at the same time move your hands in the same, vague pattern that he used. Again, the child will feel understood on a non-verbal level, and you can go on to sort out the confusion you have spotted.

You can also utilize your child's movement-gesture patterns by working to improve his use of them. The clearer and more obvious the patterns a child uses and the more he understands other people's patterns, the better he will communicate. This is not only a case of providing more chance to practise what the child already knows; gesture patterns are not always instinctive or spontaneous, so there may have to be some actual teaching. The gesture vocabulary on this page will help. Add to it by drawing up your personal mental dictionary of useful movements because gestures differ between cultures, from region to region, from one gender to another, from one

A GESTURE VOCABULARY

Add to this vocabulary to build your child's awareness of gestures.

And so on: hand circling away from body.
Baby: crossed arms, rocking from one side to the other.
Come here: beckoning with a finger or waving a hand towards the body.
Definite: a firm downwards hand movement.
Easy: a waving movement, with arms away from body and palms open.
Flowing: a rippling movement of fingers with hand moving from left to right in front of the body.
For example: one hand out, palm outstretched.
Go away: pushing movement of hand away from the body.
Hurry: an inwards rolling movement of the hand or finger.
I: hands pointing to upper chest.
I know: finger click, raise of eyebrows.
Just this much: holding finger and thumb a small distance apart at face level.
Let's go: a sudden shift of body in one direction.
Maybe: a tilt of head, shoulders, hands.
No: head shake in some countries, nod in others.
Opposite: hand turned over repeatedly.
Positive: thumbs up.
Quiet: one finger held to mouth.
Relief: a sudden dropping movement of the body.
Sleepy: head suddenly put to one side, eyes and mouth drooping.
Stop: slightly raised hand or finger.
Time: tiny gesture towards the wrist on which watch is worn.
Unpleasant: pull-back of head, nose-wrinkle.
Vague: waving movements of hands, palms open.
Wait a minute: one finger up in front of chest, eyebrows raised.
Yes: head nod in many countries.

generation to the next. Begin by being clear and obvious about your own patterns. Watch what other people do, playing 'look at that' when sitting in a shopping centre or café.

Finally, when your child uses gestures well to make his words clearer, reward him by responding. A nod of comprehension, an 'I see!' smile, a comment that indicates understanding – all these will show a child that his body language is effective, and will encourage him to improve it even more.

CHAPTER TWO

LEARNING TO LEARN

Every child wants to learn, even those with less-than-glowing school reports. While chimpanzees explore their environment only for a particular reason – to discover food, to rediscover Mum or to find ways around that large boulder – young humans have an inner urge to learn about their world even when there is no survival need to do so. One research study showed that four-month-old babies rewarded by food for exploring will be just as eager to explore when they are full and do not need food.

The most basic form of learning is simple exploration, that inner drive to look at something and see what it can do. This could be the physical exploration of the baby and the toddler, or the mental exploration – the manipulation not of actual things but of linguistic symbols – of the child.

How do children's bodies encourage them to explore? The basics are these. Human senses are strongly attuned to pay attention to change, for that might hold a danger or an opportunity. From birth, then, your child's sensory channels respond strongly to objects and ideas that are novel or different, such as a completely new voice or a minute change in a familiar voice.

And as long as that change is unthreatening, your child will continue to want to know more about it. So first you will see all the typical signs of positive attention (*see page 16*) – 'eyes wide open . . . bright with excitement . . . watching intently . . . totally oblivious to anything else', as various questionnaire respondents described them.

Once the child has homed in on this new, or changing, thing, you will notice experimentation. All children are highly motivated by producing a response from things. Six-month-old Amy, exploring a toy, showed the physical movements of 'turning, twisting, putting it in her mouth'; two-year-old Helen while exploring water, demonstrated the more sophis-

ticated gestures of 'pouring, splashing, spilling', and twelve-year-old Andrea, exploring a science problem, showed the physical cues of imagining, thinking, postulating, surmising – 'her head was up, eyes moving, mouth working'. The aim is to create an even more novel response, which once again floods the senses with appealing stimulation. This experimentation can be either physical and literal, as the child interacts with various objects, people and events, or mental and symbolic, as the child manipulates the words and images that represent things.

The child will carry on experimenting until the novelty is gone, at which point the brain signals to the body to stop exploring and move on to something

Joy, at twelve months, explores not only by looking intently and putting objects in her mouth, but also by shaking them, turning them over and over, putting in and taking them out of containers, thus learning how things work.

Even a child of only a few months who cannot work out what something is or does, will show a concentrated frown, fixed stare and half-open mouth, as if trying to take in every possible piece of information about the object. He will then systematically try new approaches until one works, or until frustration builds to real distress, provoking howls of protest.

EXPLORATION STAGES

From birth, a child begins to explore. This chart outlines the four key stages in this process.

EXPLORATION STAGE	EXPLORATION SIGNS
At birth	Natural short-sightedness means most exploration is through touch, taste and smell, though the child explores with eyes if something is held close. Look for signs of child exploring via sight, hearing, touch, smell, taste – the sensory channels
Infant	By three months, the child has learned to focus. All five channels are used. Mouth is primary exploring tool. By six months, he has probably learned to grasp, and can manipulate objects and explore them with hands. By eight months, finger and thumb are able to work in opposition and grasp things, so hands take over from mouth as main exploring tool. Look for signs of child exploring through all the sensory channels, plus using hands
Toddler	Crawling then walking bring mobility – and new exploration opportunities. A toddler can move and carry things. Talking begins, so he can explore things by referring to them, rather than physically manipulating them. Look for signs that the child is exploring through sensory channels, hands, and signs of thinking such as eye movements
Child	Increased mobility and independence make exploration easier. Writing and reading mean mental exploration is often more important than physical. Signs of physical exploration decrease considerably by adolescence

new. The body signs will change, sometimes instantly, to ones of non-attention and disengagement. Eye contact goes, movement dies away, heart-rate decreases (or increases if the boredom is stressful), focus dies as if a light has been turned off, or as one questionnaire respondent put it, 'he looks at his feet . . . sits back . . . stares aimlessly'.

You can work with the body's natural processes to encourage your child to explore. Stimulate all five sensory channels, offering as many opportunities as possible for using them. Do not force novelty on a child; this will make her feel unsafe, and she will therefore stop the exploration. It is important to offer new stimulus, though, particularly the type that produces a positive 'attention' response. Allow time and space for the kind of experimentation where the child herself can produce a response. At the very moment when attention for one thing dies, offer something new to be explored. In particular, when the child hits a particular stage of exploration such as grasping, walking or talking, be there with lots of support and reward.

You will almost certainly have put many, if not all, of these principles into practice with your toddler already. They are also useful however if you want to support your adolescent's exploration. The exploration body language of a thirteen-year-old thinking through a maths problem may have 'gone underground', because older children explore more by thinking than by doing, but the basic principles of helping the child learn remain the same. Offer new experiences across a whole range of sensory channels; take trips, organize visits, arrange to meet new people or go to new places. This time, though, look not for wild bounces of glee when water is poured,

REWARD OR PUNISHMENT?

Another well-known key to your child's learning is whether she gets rewarded for something or not. At the most basic physiological level, what brings comfort through sensory channels is done more often, what brings discomfort or pain is done less often and intriguingly, what brings no response at all often fades from the repertoire and ceases to be done at all. Very early in your child's life, this body comfort or discomfort becomes linked to what important people like you feel and think. The baby senses this through your body language. You know instinctively how to reward and so reinforce, registering delight and offering cuddles, for example, when baby starts to babble. It is a frightening thought that, if you consistently and rigorously offered silence and a blank gaze instead, your child might never learn to talk. So be aware of how each of your movements or gestures teaches a lesson. Always ask yourself what that lesson is, and whether it is a useful one.

but much subtler, downtime cues as the concepts are jiggled in the brain. Expect a little wariness to begin with, but support your child while she encounters each new situation or experience then sit back and watch her learn.

Blocks to Exploration

What happens if the process stops? It is interesting to notice when a child is exploring, but it is utterly vital to notice if a child stops. It can happen. Studies have shown that if chimpanzees are insecure, they revert to what is called 'anti-exploratory behaviour': sitting very still and rhythmically repeating a familiar movement. Children react similarly, whether threatened by stress at school, by pressure at home, by being frowned at for trying something new, or by being forced into coping with too many novel things all at once.

At Christmas, five-year-old Katherine was playing with a new construction toy, exploring what each piece did. When her big brother rampaged through the room, walloping her as he went, and scattering the pieces, she immediately withdrew, not only

At nine months, Dorothy has mastered the delicate finger and thumb 'opposition' which allows her to manipulate things and so explore them better. She also has the advantage of a stable sitting position, although as yet her lack of mobility stops her from further exploration.

Motivation can be underpinned by negative emotions. The spectators above are motivated, but are also tense and worried. Notice the forward lean and concerned expressions of the children on the right and the little boy whose hands cover his mouth.

In the scrum (right), motivation varies. The frowns reveal the negative attitude of the boys at the back. Slight mouth movements show inner debate about joining in, while raised shoulders signify body resistance. In contrast, the expressions of the lads in front show energy and motivation.

UNMOTIVATED OR JUST UNSTIMULATED?

When a child is uninterested in learning, adults term this 'lack of motivation'. It actually means that she finds nothing sufficiently stimulating to warrant attention or exploration. Below are some typical body language signs of motivation and lack of motivation. A willing child can improve the way she feels by changing her body language from unmotivated to motivated.

	MOTIVATED	UNMOTIVATED
Example	Hannah, eight, hearing Dad tell an interesting story	Wendy, nine, listening to Dad explaining something boring
Body direction	Leaning forward to take things in better	Leaning back, tilting chair away to 'escape'
Body position	Legs pulled back underneath body allowing more alert position	Legs stretched out in front, distancing her from Dad.
Head and spine position	Upright	Slumped
Limb position	Open: arms unfolded, legs uncrossed; front-facing	Head leaning to one side resting on hand; arms folded; legs crossed
Movement	Non-fidgety rhythmic movement, often in time to what others say; leaning further forward when asked a question; 'micronods' of agreement	Tiny 'escape' movements with her feet and hands; tiny head shakes of disagreement
Eyes	Open, wide, focused, taking things in	Glazed; looking at floor or round the room; shutting things out by closing eyes
Voice	High-pitched; slightly breathless; speaks quickly; emphasizes important words	Low-pitched, or high if irritated; slow, dragged-out words
Physical functions	Increased heartbeat; breathing ready for action; good skin colour	Increased heartrate due to stress
Internal experience	Views of imagined scenes; pleasurable tummy flutters	Feeling of boredom; unpleasant tension in her muscles when she wants to move but cannot

backing behind a protective sofa, but going very quiet. 'She gazed into space for a few minutes, then started moving the bits again, but this time very simply, putting one on top of the other and taking them off again. She did this for quite a while. Eventually, she started to play as before.' In place of excited, positive attention behaviour, Katherine's Dad noticed seemingly blocked sensory channels. In place of the busy hand-and-eye movements of experimentation, she showed small, close-to-the-body gestures that demonstrated fear of trying anything different, with a static, fixed gaze that showed a wariness of imagining anything new.

If this happens to your child – and after a big scare, she might stop exploring for a long time – do not panic. Remember firstly that, for children, exploring is the natural option. It is only insecurity that stops a child learning. When security returns she will revert to type and start exploring again immediately. Secondly, remember that you are almost certainly the main source of security in your child's world, and you know instinctively how to help.

Does your child know what the source of worry is? If so, use all your skills to solve the short-term problem of the scary sister or the longer-term problem of the critical teacher. If neither of you know what the matter is, then assume that her body has gained the impression that exploring is dangerous, and is giving the child internal danger signals every time she tries. Your job is to concentrate on making it safe to explore by reducing the pain. Reassure. Give permission to fail. Provide opportunities for safe exploration with no risk of getting it wrong. Do not rush in yourself, as the physiological feel-good factor for the child is knowing that she produces the response. And always reward exploration behaviour with smiles and hugs for its own sake, not just for what it produces. Given time, you will have a ten-year-old who is as thrilled by learning as is your one-year-old.

Modelling Magic

When it comes to learning, children have an in-built advantage. Rather than wasting time learning every-

By just a few weeks old, a baby can accurately copy (or model) a variety of movements, including opening his mouth, sticking his tongue out and pouting. He finds this amusing and stimulating, but likes it even better when he repeats a movement and the willing adult copies the action.

thing from scratch, children take the short cut – they copy. When your child sees another person, for example, all her sensory channels will be on full-attention alert. She takes in what she senses and stores away the possibility of reproducing it as exactly as possible. It is an impressive 'modelling machine'.

The machine instinctively models what catches its attention most. This is usually people. A nine-minute-old baby will make a stronger neurological response to a human face than to any other stimulus. Within the next two months she will make a clear body response to two eye-like circles drawn on a card (but not to single or triple circles). By seven months, particular people become more interesting, and more modell-able, than others. This may be someone familiar but, as the child gets older, and nature is less concerned about bonding her to you alone, a new person may well become the focus of attention. I once spent an hour-long car journey sitting next to an enthralled nine-month-old who gazed at me unblinking – a miniature human vacuum cleaner craving all the input this new person, with her new behaviours and appearance, could bring.

The modelling machine does not simply take in

MODELLING PHYSICAL FUNCTIONS

Children are capable of modelling quite detailed physical functions. This chart shows what even a toddler will unconsciously take in when seeing you cope with a tense situation. The example used here describes what happens when a large dog approaches you in the street.

FUNCTION	DETAIL	CONTEXT
Distance	Where you position yourself; how near or far; how you move towards or away	How close you go to the dog; whether you stay upright or bend down; whether you move towards the dog or pull back in fear
Posture	Spine angle; head angle; muscle tension; how hands and feet are placed	How tense your spine is; the angle at which you hold your head to see the dog, and how this changes as you assess the dog's intentions
Movement	Which movement is used and where; shape, speed, direction, pace, rhythm	How and at what speed you reach out a hand; whether or not you step back when the dog barks
Expression	Forehead lines; shape of mouth; nose wrinkle; face shape	Whether you smile confidently or look anxious as you approach the dog
Eyes	Direction and length of gaze; pupil size; lid and brow movement; blink rate	Whether or not you look at the dog directly; how your pupils dilate or contract to indicate attraction or not; whether or not you blink in nervousness, and how this changes as the dog moves
Voice	Volume, speed, rhythm, pace, pitch, stress on particular words	Whether your voice is low and relaxed, or high, quick and nervous, and how this changes as the dog gets nearer
Touch	Where you touch; how firmly; how quickly; with what rhythm	Whether or not you pat the dog firmly, and how this changes as the dog responds to your pat; what happens if the dog moves suddenly
Physical functions	Breathing rate; heartrate; blood pressure; skin-colour change	Whether your breathing speeds up or slows down; how your skin colour changes with your emotions as the dog licks your hand

information from external stimulus. It also remembers and stores what is happening internally. A child notes another person's movements or voice tone, but also picks up on that person's heartbeat, breathing rate and even adrenalin production. The result is that the child will also imitate emotions, as any stressed and harassed parent with a telepathically-screaming baby will testify.

Much modelling goes on beneath the surface; we have no idea of exactly what the modelling machine is taking in. But the external proof of success is a child's ability to reproduce what he has modelled. A child can do this startlingly early in life: seven-hour-old children can reproduce the action of an adult sticking his tongue out – and with incredible precision. One study shows that copying between child and adult can happen within one forty-eighth of a second.

In general, the more unconscious and instinctive the element the child is modelling, the more likely he is to replicate it spontaneously and precisely. Conversely, deliberate elements are the least instinctive. So while two-year-old Sam may well be fascinated by Mum's sketch of a sailing boat, he cannot consciously copy the drawing, though he will have a good try at holding the pencil. If, however, Mum cries when she has had bad news, Sam may well reproduce her physical state completely, down to the breathing pattern as well as the tears.

When the child reproduces what he has modelled, the result is usually an immediate positive response from those around. Few things motivate a child more than a response, so he reproduces the behaviour again, gets another delighted reaction, and does his trick once again. By the time the novelty has worn off, the behaviour is part of his in-built repertoire.

COPYING FOR CLOSENESS

Matching your child's body language as accurately as you can will not only help you to learn about your child; the similarity created will also bring you closer. This chart shows you how.

EXAMPLE	HOW TO MATCH
Your new-born, sleeping	Lie quietly with your baby next to you. Curl in the same position. Imagine your world consists of touch, smell and taste. Breathe once for every two or three of the baby's breaths. What is your experience?
Your toddler, fretting	Stand or sit as you see your toddler doing. Hold your head in the same position. Fiddle with your hands in the same way. Make your voice as sad and whiney. What do you understand now about your child's feelings?
Your three-year-old, painting	Copy the broad, uncontrolled brush strokes that your child uses. Be deliberately unco-ordinated. What does it tell you about painting as a three-year-old?
Your four-year-old, exploring the garden	Sit or lie fairly low down. Copy the wide-eyed attention of the child. Listen to what he would hear at this level. Feel the foliage in the same ways. What do you imagine your child thinks?
Your five-year-old, learning to write	Sit in the same position as your child. Copy hand movements, facial tension, any nervous ticks. Let these movements get you in touch with the feeling that writing is difficult. What do you now realize your child needs?

Selective Learning

What if your child models something that you do not want him to, learning eagerly the very things you abhor? There are five ways to stop this:
1. Block or remove the input so the child's body cannot copy.
2. Make the copied behaviour less stimulating and therefore less attractive.
3. Make the person being modelled less important than other models.

4. Fail to respond to (that is, genuinely ignore) the behaviour when it is shown.

5. Stop the child from reproducing the modelled behaviour.

Some solutions suggested by experts in child-rearing pick up on the final suggestion, punishing the child for reproducing the behaviour. This, however, is the psychological equivalent of barring the stable door after the horse has bolted. The external signs may cease, but the body has already absorbed the body language, and it will remain available for life.

It is better to use one of the first four solutions. Try blocking or removing the input: if your child is learning to swear from friends, get together with other parents and start a 'neighbourhood watch'. If

The class is modelling in all three channels. They look at and copy the teacher, take their aural cue from the piano music and are helped kinaesthetically by the teacher himself holding them in the right position so that they can store the correct internal feeling in their kinaesthetic channels.

blocking or removal is impossible, make the behaviour less rewarding than other behaviours, or reward other behaviours more than the problem one: give a hug or a favour every time he is tempted to swear but restrains himself. Make the people the child is modelling from less important in the child's life; try introducing other, non-swearing friends who are more fun or let him overhear his favourite uncle or brother saying how childish swearing is. Finally, try genuinely ignoring his swearing; initially he may swear even more to get a response from you but, as the main reason for swearing is to get attention, he may simply forget to do so if there is no response.

What should you do when you want a child to learn something, and he simply does not? Your toddler might not quite be able, for example, to use a knife and fork. Is this because there are insufficient new and different models of what should be done? Do you show him how, point out to him what other children are doing, talk about the problems? Is it because the person offered as a model is not important enough in his life (he never sees you use cutlery as you are always busy feeding him at mealtimes)? Are you giving a sufficiently strong response to when he approaches success (or is he getting more attention from you when he fails than when he succeeds)?

If a child has not mastered a skill, never assume that nothing has been modelled. Something always has been. Even though your child may not have learned how to use the toilet, he has certainly learned, from the teaching process you initiated, how to become tense, worried and fearful, or calm, laid-back and self-accepting.

Matching and Leading

If you want to give your child a helping hand in modelling something specific, consider this. The gap between what a child and an adult can do is often just too great for the child to begin to imitate. Sam, mentioned earlier, was able to hold the pencil but not draw the picture. In these situations, make a bridge between the child's skill level and yours.

This bridge consists of consciously 'matching' or copying what the child does. You then continue to follow his actions up to the point where he will follow you into a slightly improved version of what he was doing. This technique will not work with big differences in skill; Sam's Mum could match him for hours but could never lead him into drawing an adult-level yacht. And it will work better with simple skills,

such as holding a pencil, than with complex skills such as copying a whole picture.

The trick is to match your child's behaviour as accurately as you can in order to give him a chance of identifying with what you are doing. Make all the elements you can consciously control, such as movement, posture, gesture and even breathing, as close to the child's as possible. Your movement patterns will still be more advanced than his but when you are 'following' his lead, with your movements now only marginally different, the child may copy you and so spontaneously do what you want him to. And if at this point you copy his new and more effective behaviour he will be delighted and naturally create his own internal reward for having modelled you.

Formal Learning

Not all learning is as instinctive and natural as exploration or modelling. By the time your child reaches school age, she will also be learning more formally. From you, an older child or a play-school teacher, she will have picked up the ability to take in 'presented information' or to accept instruction. At this point, as your role as her teacher begins to lessen, you can use body-language principles not only to find out what works for her, but also to check that her formal learning is going well.

In general, look for enthusiastic and positive body language when she is learning, whether observed by you in the classroom, revising or doing homework. As well as the attention signs mentioned on page 18, check the body signs of thinking explained on page 22. If they simply do not happen and the child remains too still with too little eye movement, the chances are that no learning is taking place.

The signs may also reveal confusion. Take Rose, aged ten, who was trying to understand the markings on a local district map. A first glance made no sense, so she then 'gave a rapid, flicking eye movement', which showed her desperately searching around all her thinking channels to find one that made sense of what she was trying to understand. The questionnaire response also commented on her 'little intakes of

These girls are learning through different channels. The girl in black checks what she has to do through visual input. The girl in red listens to instructions – see her head and jaw angle. The girl in green learns kinaesthetically, as revealed by her downward glance and pressure on the barre.

Good early learning combines all thinking channels. Children have the chance to look and draw (visual channel), to speak and listen (auditory channel), do hands-on work with paper and blocks (kinaesthetic channel) and to form their own words internally, then write them down (digital).

breath'; a disturbed, irregular breathing pattern often indicates that a child is finding the processing of information difficult. Once Rose had the map key explained, and had taken her time to go through and thoroughly understand the code, she then showed a very typical 'nod, and a breath out . . .'. This demonstrated that she had successfully mentally processed, checked and understood through her thinking channels the information that her sensory channels were taking in.

To examine learning effectiveness more specifically, also check whether your child is getting the most out of each kind of learning style. The chart on page 39 lists some common ways of teaching in Western schools. Check the indicators given against what your child does. With luck, all the signs will indicate that she is learning well. If not, you may want to help her with extra practice in taking in or processing information in that particular style.

The ideal in education is to present every piece of information in as many ways as possible. Most

THE SIGNS OF LEARNING

When learning is happening most effectively, certain body-language signs are in evidence. This *chart outlines four types of learning and which signs might be present for each of the four.*

	TALK-BASED OR MUSIC-BASED LEARNING	VISUAL, IMAGE-BASED LEARNING	HANDS-ON, EXPERIENTIAL LEARNING	WRITTEN-WORD LEARNING
Example	Drama class; learning a poem with music	Maths class involving a drawing of a triangle	Pottery	Comprehension exercise
Main channel	What is heard: words and music	What is seen	What is directly felt	The way the words sound in child's head
The child mainly pays attention to . . .	Words and sounds (also teacher's appearance)	The sight of the triangle (plus sound of the teacher's words)	The feel of clay (plus sight of pot)	Internal sound of words (plus how they look on paper)
Child stores the learning as . . .	Mental words, and images created by words; mental picture of teacher	Detailed mental pictures, mental words	A mental touch memory	Mental 'tape' of the words; image of words on paper; images created by words
Signs of learning well	Head on one side; tiny, rhythmic head movements	Head up; eyes wide and focused; slight nod at a meaningful image	Leaning forwards slightly; exploring and checking with hands	Leaning head to one side; tiny movements of lips or throat
When answering a question will . . .	Quote what has been said, or pick up on the rhythm of words	Accompany words with hand movements to reflect triangle shape	Accompany words with hand movements	Often hesitate as if listening to sound of the mental voice
When revising or recalling work will . . .	Look to the side, left or right; speak or write phrases used	Look up; defocus; raise eyebrows; sketch out details	Look down; want to demonstrate movements	Look down; say the words to self 'in throat', silently and with minimal movement
Make sure learning or revision includes . . .	Saying words aloud that have to be learned	Drawing, preferably with colour	Hands-on practice	Speaking and writing words to be learned

teachers do this: talking to the class, using pictures, facilitating discussion, providing opportunities to 'do'. It is possible, however, that you or your child's teachers are concentrating on one particular style. This can limit the thinking channels used and the lessons learned. I heard of one four-year-old who went to a play school where talking and music were encouraged, but there were no pictures on the walls. Another thirteen-year-old reported a history teacher who, every day for a year, came in, said 'Good morning,' wrote notes on the board in silence, said 'Good afternoon,' and went out. No discussion was allowed, so the teacher was ignoring one of the key ways children have of consolidating information:

hearing themselves and others talk, and integrating what is said into their digital thinking channel.

What if a plea to the teacher for 'more pictures . . . more words . . . more chance to practise' falls on deaf ears? You may have to take things into your own hands. Look at the range of possible learning styles on the chart, and see how you could reconstruct them at home. If your child learns best through pictures, get her to draw out what she has been taught that day. If talking about something is the best way to learn, get her to tell you about her lessons. If hands-on experience is lacking, provide extra practice.

When your child joins the school system, you may hit whole new areas of concern because, as children

A SPELLING STRATEGY

Research shows that students who spell well do so by remembering visually. They mentally 'see' a word, up and to their left (or right if left-handed), often as bright letters on a dark background. Try these steps if your child has difficulty spelling.

● Get him to deliberately look up and to his left, and imagine a big, bright poster. Ask for a detailed description of what that poster looks like: how big, how bright?
● Tell him to imagine a simple word that he can already spell, like 'cat', on that poster. Get him to spell out the letters, first forwards, then backwards, to check he can 'see' the word.
● Run through this with him twenty times with more and more difficult words, spelling forwards and backwards.
● If he has difficulty with any word, get him to make the sign clearer, bigger, brighter.
● Repeat the exercise regularly until the child does it spontaneously with every new or difficult word he learns.

grow, their learning usually becomes more structured and formal. Darren, aged two, runs happily around the room to discover interesting things and show them to Dad. His brother Stephen, at eleven, has to sit still and compete with thirty others for teachers' attention. The younger child can indicate clearly with his body language what interests or puzzles him; the older child has to follow formal body-language rules for getting attention, such as hand-raising. The toddler initiates and interacts in order to learn constantly, while the secondary-school student can spend as much as eighty-four per cent of his time not interacting.

This kind of formality may cause all kinds of non-verbal problems. A child who learns best while moving his body – even minutely – may suddenly have many of his modes of learning disrupted. Accurate non-verbal communication between teacher and student may start to go astray. Children with more dominant or disruptive body language get interaction of a negative kind, while the child whose body language is less demanding can sometimes miss out completely.

How can this process be sidestepped? Studies of American and European children who get the most out of formal learning have shown some consistent

GOOD TEACHER OR BAD?

Studies have shown consistent non-verbal differences both in what young people see as good teaching, and in what gives them effective learning. Check out your child's teachers against this comparison chart.

Good teacher
Likes and is likeable
- Gives smiles and eye contact.
- Stands close, bends to compensate for height difference.
- Nods approval of what students say and do.

Is confident, in control
- Stands tall, is relaxed.
- Laughs; encourages genuine, non-mocking laughter.
- Spots disruption through body language signals – acts instantly.

Creates interest in the subject
- Varies facial expression.
- Uses gestures often and clearly to explain topic.
- Leans forward, excitedly, when explaining something.

Bad teacher
Shows dislike and is disliked
- Hides behind the barrier of the desk.
- Has closed body positions.
- Never touches students.

Is unconfident, loses control
- Shows nervousness in ticks and blinks.
- Has tense voice that breaks or stutters.
- Does not notice challenging body language.

Creates boredom in the subject
- Has monotonous voice – students hate this.
- Moves about very little in classroom.
- Shows micromovements of boredom or anger.

The secondary group in the picture above is obviously eager to learn. This shows through their upright postures and hands, focused gaze and evidence of very little distraction. They are helped by their teacher's clear gesture, open posture, eye contact and approving expression. In contrast, notice the obvious weariness of the primary class (left), with slumped postures, yawns, lid-rubbing, loss of eye contact and fidgeting. This is paralleled – and possibly increased – by their teacher's slumped and head-lowered downtime reading position.

Whatever the central boy's question (above), the teacher certainly finds it threatening. Both the boy's friends comfort themselves with hand-to-mouth gestures, while the blond lad looks down as if to distance himself from any potential trouble. For a moment, teacher and pupil lock eyes, but the adult's head and body angle combine with his gaze in a display of dominance that 'stares down' the boy. The teacher has re-established authority (right). The culprit has taken on an appeasement posture, looking smaller by withdrawing and hunching shoulders, but with some resentment in eyes and mouth. Both his classmates feel safe enough to look up and interact again.

patterns. You can help your child to develop these in order to achieve both teacher approval and classroom success; the chances are that he will enjoy school more, too. As always, these skills only work if they come from genuine willingness; if used with a naughty gleam in the eye, they will fall flat. (Please note that many of the suggestions made here contradict respectful body language in Eastern countries and so will not be effective there.)

The first step is to make the teacher feel good, about herself and her teaching. This simply involves letting her know, non-verbally, when something appeals. Body language works particularly well here because giving verbal compliments to superiors is often seen as forward or cheeky. A child is usually aware of when a teacher has explained something well during a science lesson, or made an interesting point in history. If he then allows that awareness to show as a genuinely positive expression – leaning forward towards the teacher when she is speaking; continued and interested eye contact – then he has found non-threatening ways of telling the teacher that she is approved of. The result will be a more relaxed teacher, better teaching and a greater inclination to interact with the approving student to give help, support and praise.

Admiration

When a teacher praises a child, the successful student has a non-verbal way of encouraging it to happen again: smiling and looking directly at the teacher. This, once again, makes the teacher feel good and more likely to praise the child next time. In a neat and beneficial body-language circle, student and teacher form a mutual admiration society.

A child who gets the most out of learning also has an innate ability to use the body language of confident understanding. Assuming a still posture, with the open eyes or 'pricked' ears of positive attention signals, often indicates 'intelligent' to a teacher. One questionnaire respondent called this her daughter's 'intent look'. When the child understands something, he can clearly show this non-verbally by nodding his head or breathing out deeply. The teacher will increasingly think of him as a bright student, and treat him accordingly. The fact is that, although most teachers consciously pay attention to the less bright pupils in the class, unconsciously their favourable body language is aimed at those who seem to understand them.

HOMEWORK ERGONOMICS

Bodies suffer in the wrong environment and that affects the mind. Set up the right conditions for your child's home learning.

- Space: check the room the child works in. Is it so cramped that it feels constricting or so large that it feels insecure?
- Room to move: sitting still can lead to demotivating slumping; occasional movement gets adrenalin going.
- Posture: do desk and chair let the child think in all channels by easily positioning body, head and eyes?
- Sound: is there quiet for word work? Is there optional noise, used for blocking off 'internal dialogue' if the child needs to concentrate only on what she sees or feels.
- Touch: are work surfaces and chair supportive; are they the right height; are they relaxing, but not sleep-inducing?

What if a child does not understand? Has he got to pretend to comprehend in order to keep the teacher on his side? Is there not a danger in this strategy of his not learning simply because the teacher thinks he knows it all? Studies suggest otherwise. A child who seems bright and interested may actually get more help if he hits a problem than his less obviously intelligent class-mate does. And he can add to his chances of getting help by signalling in a particular way if he needs it. He will get willing and extended support by sitting still until he catches the teacher's eye, looking quietly puzzled, asking for clarification with an interested voice tone. Interestingly, a slight frown, mentioned by more than one questionnaire respondent as a sign that their children did not comprehend, also gives an appearance of concentration and willingness, and typically gets a positive response. Conversely, consider the child who switches off attention when confused; looks at friends for help rather than the teacher; 'fidgets . . . moves about . . . moves her eyes from side to side . . . does not sit still'; seems angry rather than puzzled; asks sullenly or challengingly for an answer. He will often be ignored, disciplined, or given unwilling help. The lesson, as always, is that children who offer positive body language will almost invariably attract a positive response.

CHAPTER THREE

EMOTIONS

Babies react strongly to real-life problems such as hunger, cold and pain. This reaction has one aim only: to get support from you, the nearest adult. If you do not appear at once, then the external danger signals get louder and stronger until you cannot ignore them. This is because the baby's internal alarm bells are also getting louder. If new-born Julia is cold – a life-threatening event for a small baby – her kinaesthetic channel is at full stretch. It generates all kinds of feelings: surface sensations of heat or cold, pressure or pain; deeper sensations from her muscles; uncomfortable feelings from her internal organs. She waves her arms and legs frantically and lets out a howl of anguish. It hurts inside, she continues to howl until help arrives.

It is understandable that such real-life events cause strong reactions. But human beings also get strong internal reactions to events that are not directly physical in origin: mental events, such as looking forward to something, or even the words that symbolize such events. Studies have shown that just the thought of an event that involves strong sensation will send electrical impulses in the brain, producing a physical reaction. We call these strong internal reactions emotions: anger, fear, surprise, delight. The child experiences them through the kinaesthetic channel in a jolt of sensation. They are also accompanied, whether the child is aware of it or not, by a mental picture, sound or words, which trigger that jolt of emotion through a memory, a realization or perhaps a fantasy about the future (*see page 20*).

So while a four-year-old chimp will only get angry if something physically threatens it, four-year-old Abigail can be equally affected if Dad says, 'We are not going to Nanny's today.' These words will make her think about times in the past when she has gone to Nanny's, perhaps through an unconscious picture of Nanny's face or the memory of her voice. These thoughts in turn will generate angry feelings about the possibility of that never happening again. She may become aware of a tingling in her hands and feet; a tightening of her back muscles; feelings of warmth, movement and contraction in her tummy as it fizzes with anger. It may be 'just an emotion', but the internal body language is very real, as is the temper tantrum that results from it.

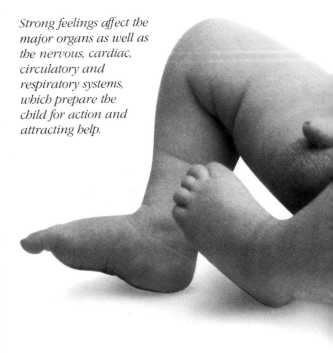

Strong feelings affect the major organs as well as the nervous, cardiac, circulatory and respiratory systems, which prepare the child for action and attracting help.

Showing Emotions

Children do not show every human emotional signal from the day they are born. This led to the general belief that children learn external emotional expression as they grow up. The implication of this was that emotions might be expressed differently by different cultures. Then Charles Darwin (1809–82) drew up a list of sixteen questions about emotional expressions which he distributed through church missionaries all over the world. The results proved his suspicion that emotions were instinctive, the same for everyone, regardless of where or how they were brought up. All over the world, a sulking child will stick her lower lip forward in what we call a 'pout'. This makes sense. From birth, a child has to be able to communicate her feelings to any adult who can help, not just one with the same background.

The reason why babies do not show all the emotional signs at birth is probably because they do not develop all the emotions until later in life. Emotional development takes place through a combination of methods based on instinct, modelling of other people's emotions, and learning or unlearning of the emotions you encourage or discourage.

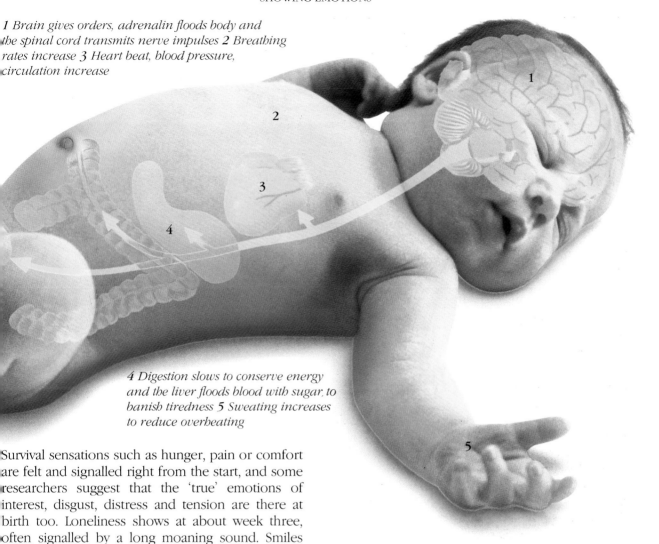

1 Brain gives orders, adrenalin floods body and the spinal cord transmits nerve impulses 2 Breathing rates increase 3 Heart beat, blood pressure, circulation increase

4 Digestion slows to conserve energy and the liver floods blood with sugar to banish tiredness 5 Sweating increases to reduce overheating

Survival sensations such as hunger, pain or comfort are felt and signalled right from the start, and some researchers suggest that the 'true' emotions of interest, disgust, distress and tension are there at birth too. Loneliness shows at about week three, often signalled by a long moaning sound. Smiles appear at about six weeks when a baby is ready to form emotional bonds and begin to explore in earnest. And although a young baby can be startled or surprised, it takes a while for real fear of other people to develop. Finally, while frustration can appear at only a few weeks, angry crying and yelling seems to appear only after the fifth month, along with sadness, repulsion and joy.

As they get older, children become more able to signal emotion but they choose to do so less and less. This is not only because adults discourage strong displays of emotion, it is also the body's response to the fact that older children can look after themselves better and ask for help with words. As this happens, the external signs diminish naturally. We do need to be aware, however, that the internal signs are still there. The chart on pages 46–7 lists these external signals and what may be happening for the child on the inside.

DEVELOPING EMOTIONAL RECOGNITION

● Give her an emotional vocabulary by teaching her to name the emotions she sees in others.
● Tell her honestly about your emotions; help her calibrate what she sees with what you feel.
● Use the emotional models on television or video to help her make body-language distinctions. Ask questions such as 'What is the actor feeling . . . how is he feeling now . . . how do you know?'
● Draw her attention to the eyes, eyebrows and mouth as studies show that most emotional signals are communicated via these features.
● Give your child a vocabulary to describe what she feels inside. Use direct words such as 'heavy . . . moving . . . warm', or metaphors such as 'butterflies in my tummy. After a burst of emotion, get her to describe how it felt.

EMOTION-WATCHING	FEAR	DISGUST
American anthropologist Paul Ekman showed photos of facial expressions to people from the USA, Brazil, Chile, Argentina and Japan. He identified six basic emotions that were recognized in much the same way almost all over the world. This chart lists some of the typical signs of these emotions.	Instinctive fear develops at eight months, with 'stranger anxiety' then develops into 'realistic fear', triggered only by a true threat	The pullback response to something safe but unacceptable is there at birth, but develops fully in toddlerhood
	Eyes and eyebrows	
	Eyes open, tense, with lower lid raised; a direct stare or sideways glance, a remnant of tribal 'intruder spotting'. Eyebrows raised and drawn together as protection	Lower eyelid pushed up, to shut out the disgusting sight. Eyebrows are lowered, again to reduce vision
	Mouth	
	Open; lips drawn back tightly as if in retreat; a younger child may scream, an older one gasp	Screwed up, lower lip pulled down; emits a croaking 'ugh' sound as if the child is starting to vomit
	Nose	
		A wrinkling movement as if to block nostrils
	Body position	
	Inward and curled for self-protection; monkeys use this position to signal fear of a stronger animal; a younger child will run to you, an older one may lean towards you	Pulled back; a younger child will jerk away, jump back. An older child may show a reflex jerk of the head backwards and downwards
	Breathing	
	Becomes more rapid	Becomes more rapid
	Skin colour	
	Pale as blood rushes to protect vital organs	Pale, slightly greenish tinge if child is nauseous
	What the child feels	
	Trembling 'butterflies' in stomach; shaky and cold inside; tension; faster heartbeat; need to go to the toilet	A stomach 'churn' or 'clench'; increased saliva, a response to nausea

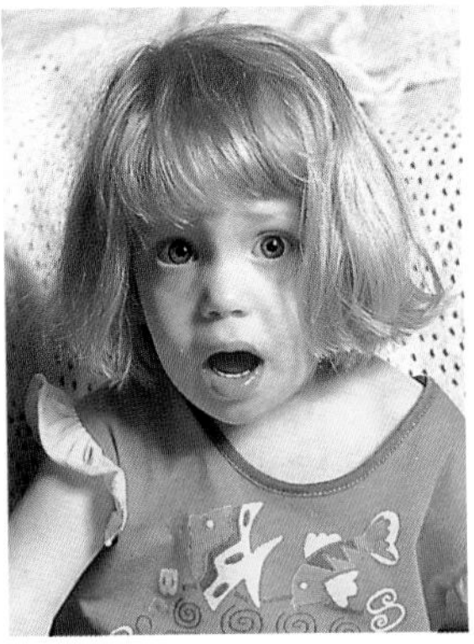

Fear

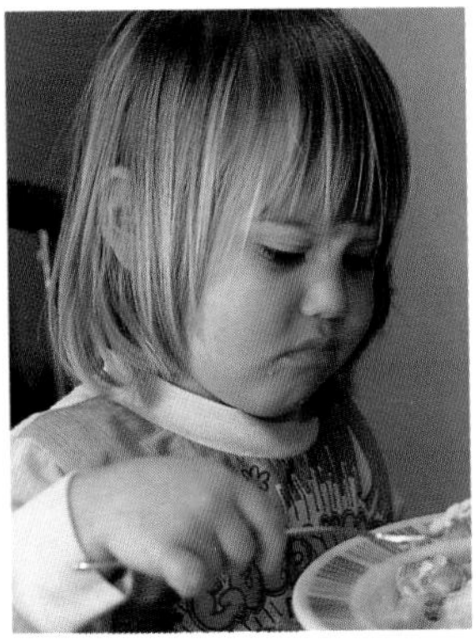

Disgust

Sadness

Surprise

Anger

Happiness

SADNESS	SURPRISE	ANGER	HAPPINESS
A basic emotion, though one of its key signs – tears – is a common emotional release for children even when they are not sad at all	The emotional reaction to something startling. It can be mixed with fear, but once surprise is identified, it can be reason for relieved smiles	Signs of real anger develop early in life, though the expression of anger is controlled – through adult 'disciplining' – equally early	The positive version of anger. Body responses prepare child for action. If child moves to contentment, signals tone down
Eyes and eyebrows			
Upper eyelids lowered; tears or gleam of moisture along lower eyelid; sunken eyes; reddening or puffiness of eyes. Eyebrows raised, to allow tears to come more easily	Eyes flick open wide to take in what is happening; pupils dilate for the same reason. Eyebrows raised and furrowed, to see better	Penetrating gaze, to 'stare down' the opposition. Eyebrows lowered and drawn together; in monkeys, this indicates the urge to attack	Eyes wide, to see good things better, or wrinkled to show a genuine smile; moisture or tears of happiness. Eyebrows lowered if laughter follows, raised if tears come
Mouth			
Downturned; lips pulled in towards each other. Lower lip trembles, a precursor of howls of grief	Jaw drops, opening mouth as it goes; a yell or gasp may be followed by breathing out or giggles of relief	Lips pushed forward as if advancing on the enemy, or parted, to let out screams, yells or hisses	Smiles or laughs; lips pulled up and back; voice is often higher than usual; words tumble out
Nose			
		Flared nostrils, a remnant of primate threatening behaviour	
Body position			
Dropping downwards with shoulders dropped, spine slumped, centre of body curled in on itself. Movement is minimal and becomes heavy and slow	A fearful backwards movement followed by a slight forwards movement to explore further; an older child may show only a slight lift of the head and shoulders	Active and alert, ready to attack or frozen with fury. Shoulders hunched in self-defence; back stiff with aggression. With younger children violent movement towards objects and people	Toddlers rush to share happiness by moving their whole body and hugging; an older child may still bounce up and down; an early adolescent may 'jiggle' head and neck
Breathing			
Rate slows; rises if sobbing begins	Becomes more rapid	Rapid and deep	Rapid and high at first, becoming deep, calm and regular
Skin colour			
Pale with redness around eyes and mouth if crying	Pale if wary, turning to warmer colour if surprise is pleasant	Pale as nervous system is stimulated; skin flushes as the nervous system calms down	Rush of blood gives good colour
What the child feels			
Heavy in tummy or across shoulders; warm prickliness around eyes; throat and nose choked	A short, sharp jolt to the tummy; a brief, faster heartbeat and rush of adrenalin; then relaxation or tears of relief	A faster heartbeat; dry mouth; faintness as blood rushes to the brain; a rush of energy to tummy or chest, spreading to hands and feet	Nervous 'butterflies', high in midriff; tingling warmth in hands and feet; relaxation down back and tummy; warm sensation in body

HOW TO HELP YOUR CHILD FEEL BETTER

If your child's emotions are not overwhelming, then simply getting him to change his body language can convince his internal functions that things are not so bad.

Begin when a child is not feeling negative. Choose an appropriate low-key positive emotion, such as 'calm' or 'content'. Ask him to remember a time when he felt quietly calm or maybe to remember someone he knows or has seen on television who felt that way. Make sure he has a clear picture and voice tone in his head as a model. How does 'calm' look? Can he copy the way 'calm' stands, sits, holds his head or mouth? In particular, get the child to copy the eye and mouth positions of 'calm'. Keep it brief and do not over-rehearse. Before finishing, ask the child to imagine that the next time he feels bad, he can 'think and act calm'. Soon he will play the game for himself, with no prompting.

Oscar, recovering from a sulk. His gaze is down, his hands hide his face and shut out the world. As he starts to recover, his arms recreate the comforting swaddling effect reminiscent of the womb, his eyes scan in an animal-like watch for danger. Feeling better, his spine straightens, and finally his focus moves outwards to uptime. Although he still pouts, he is probably nearly ready to interact again.

Reading Emotions

Children need to recognize emotions just as much as adults do. Why? When young chimps sense each other's distress, they rush to the nearest adult for protection or they do not survive long. Humankind, too, seems to have evolved to favour those who can recognize emotion in others. Studies with children aged from eight to eleven years show that those who can spot and interpret feelings are actually more popular with their class-mates.

Children can recognize distress right from birth, probably because it is such an important skill. Even a new-born baby will become upset if others are crying, probably hearing the change in voice tone and heartbeat, possibly even smelling a change in body odour. As a child grows and starts to put more distance between herself and other people, emotional signals tend to be less dependent on smell or touch and more on sight and sound, usually expression and voice tone. By six months your child can recognize an 'angry face', and at seven months will react very differently to that face as opposed to a 'happy' one. By five years of age she can easily model the body language of anger, fear and sadness, and gets naturally more and more skilled at recognizing emotions as she grows.

Giving Support

How can you help if your child is feeling down, or offer support if he is feeling good? Here I am not talking about overwhelming emotion, which I deal with later in this chapter, but the normal emotional ups and downs of day-to-day life with your child.

The first and by far the most important consideration is how you are feeling, as a child is genetically programmed to take his distress cues from those around him. If you are irritated or frustrated, even if you verbally deny your feelings, your child will pick that up and model it. If you are calm, relaxed and genuinely untroubled by the child's behaviour, his body will instinctively interpret this as 'there is actually nothing to worry about', lowering his heart-rate and relaxing him. So before even going close, relax, take deep breaths, tense your muscles and then fully loosen them, and think of other times when you have been calm.

Remember that the original survival purpose of emotional reactions – internal and external – is to get an adult on the spot. Although a child's immediate reaction to your presence may be to shout louder – in case you have missed the point – within a very short time the child's body will instinctively decrease its panic signals, and increase them again only if your

presence does not solve the problem. The key to comfort, then, is to let the child know as fully as possible that you are there. Move close, make eye contact, touch, speak.

When emotional, the body is functioning largely through the kinaesthetic channel. So start with kinaesthetic support. You will probably instinctively begin with any reminder of that most kinaesthetically supportive place of all – the womb. So for a grizzly six-month-old, you can create physical security through a rock-solid grasp, maybe even adding in a light 'swaddling' blanket to add extra holding power and therefore comfort. Conversely, an emotionally excited baby may need a series of shorter hugs that involve more body movement. For both happy and unhappy babies, use rocking movements that remind the child of the swaying it experienced in the womb when Mum walked. Hold the child next to your heart so he can hear the beat, and add a similarly rhythmic humming or 'there, there' sound. Never try simply to impose calm on a baby; he will simply increase his cries for help, feeling that you have failed to notice his distress. Instead, match his movements and rhythms first, then gradually calm him down.

An older child may pull back from an all-embracing hug. If so, whether he is deliriously happy or just in a sulk, you can create the same supportive effect with one hand rhythmically patting his back. Many emotions are experienced in organs clustered around a child's 'midline', marked by the spine, and one way to reassure is to touch that part of the body lightly, at the back, where he is less likely to feel attacked or intruded upon.

When he will not accept any touch, then a regular movement that he can see or hear (preferably matching his movements or breathing) will calm him, even if you have to pat your own hand or exaggerate your breathing within his field of vision. Watch out for signs that reveal which type of internal thought (sight, sound, internal dialogue) might be triggering the emotion most (*see page 22*). Let this inform not only your questions, but also whether you concentrate on communicating through touch, sound or sight. From that point on, as one questionnaire respondent said about her daughter, 'I make eye contact with her, be there for her when she needs me . . . but let her lead the way.'

When Emotions Conflict

When a child feels a single emotion, even a distressing one, it is straightforward to deal with. But if a child feels conflicting emotions – is 'incongruent' – then her whole physiology may literally be in opposition.

The main cause of incongruence is what children learn as they grow. A new-born baby will be utterly congruent, feeling a single emotion throughout his body, even if for only a few seconds at a time. But as children get older we give them verbal and non-verbal messages about their feelings, looking embarrassed when a boy gets tearful, shushing a girl whose voice gets angry. These additional messages may well be internalized, cropping up perhaps as a critical 'internal dialogue' in the digital thinking channel or negative feelings in the kinaesthetic channels. Both of these have a direct effect on the child's physical state. A child may therefore feel one emotion, become frightened of feeling it, be angry about feeling it. The result can be a Molotov cocktail of emotions.

It is fairly obvious why incongruence makes a child feel bad inside. Take the example of eight-year-old James. He wants to go on the school trip but is afraid to do so, and is also ashamed to show his fear. The internal signals of excitement, fear and guilt chase each other round his nervous system in a physiological tag race, literally unbalancing him. This will result in problematic behaviour on the outside; James may alternate between smiles and sulks until you and he are driven to distraction. James's incongruence may also have long-term bad effects. His conflicting body language may not only confuse you as he flips from one emotion to another but it can also distress you. Common long-term responses of those living with strongly incongruent people include stomach ulcers, chronic back tension and allergic reactions. Incongruence can also lead to James being alienated socially. Studies have shown, for example, that children who present a positive emotional expression but show micromovements of facial negativity are rated as 'untrustworthy' both by other children and by adults.

It can be even more dangerous if you turn all this on its head, where you are the one showing mixed emotions and your child is trying to cope. The child has much less power to challenge what is happening. If you are angry but try to hide that under an amused face, the child will get confused; if he then questions what is happening, 'Are you cross with me, Mummy?' and gets an embarrassed and guilty denial from you, he has four sets of non-verbal signals to cope with. In

Hayley isn't distressed, but she is incongruent. She smiles but her lips are drawn back tightly over her teeth, a sign of anxiety. Her raised shoulder 'protects' and her fingers are tense. If she were really confident with the bird, her eyes would be fully open to pay attention to it completely, whereas in fact they are slit-like, as if to keep the sight at bay.

Tom (far right) shows a different blend of emotions. He seems angry at his friends, shown by hands on hips and the flouncy walk. But there is sadness in his puffy eyes and downturned mouth. He could as easily cry as throw a tantrum.

addition, he guesses that any further interrogation will simply make things worse. When faced with this sort of denial of reality, studies have shown that children may actually develop clinical schizophrenia.

It is therefore vital for your child to be able to spot incongruence, in himself and in others. The skill is not instinctive – new-borns simply respond to the strongest emotion while toddlers often cannot tell when an adult is pretending, a fact that often leads to tears. I have commented before that observation and discussion of body language is helpful, but nowhere is this more true than with incongruence where mixed messages cause far more distress when hidden than when admitted. If you spot a child showing mixed emotions, talk to him about it. If you see influential figures, such as your child's favourite television personalities, giving mixed signals, then point it out. Finally, and most importantly, if you are incongruent, tell the child. Admitting that you feel angry even though you are trying to be calm is not a punishment for a child; it is a relief. That way he is not being asked to deny the evidence of his own eyes and ears in favour of your verbal denial.

THE SIGNS OF INCONGRUENCE

● When the actions contradict the words: calm words but clenched fist; happy words but tearful eyes; positive words but tiny shakes of the head.
● When the eyes contradict the mouth: smiling mouth but red eyes; angrily set mouth but frowning eyebrows; guiltily downcast eyes but mouth with a mischievous twist.
● When movement contradicts expression: pleasant expression but sudden irritated glare; confident expression but sideways glance of fear; stubborn expression but gleam of tears.
● When the right side contradicts the left side: head tilts one way then the other; hands, arms, shoulders perform a constant balancing act; eye movements are like those of someone watching a tennis match.
● When the body constantly contradicts itself: a rush of anger but the paralysis of fear; nervous movements caught and held still; first tantrums then tears.

HOW TO HELP YOUR INCONGRUENT CHILD

Mixed emotions need to be resolved before a child can cope with them. Here is a useful strategy.

● Physical support. Her body is in conflict with itself. Use all the non-verbal comfort signs you know to indicate safety. Once the child feels safe, her less predominant emotion may emerge, so be prepared for unexpected tears or anger.
● Information. She needs to know what is happening. Telling her that mixed emotions are natural will produce an immediate feeling of relaxation and hopefulness, even amid distress.
● Externalization. Pretend that different non-verbal communications have different 'voices'. Ask 'What is your fist saying? . . . What are your tears telling us?' Imagining that tears can talk seems strange to adults, but children often find it totally natural.
● Resolution. Talk and action are usually needed to remove the cause of conflicting emotion. You must, however, resolve all the strong feelings, not just one of them. Check continually that she is expressing – and that you are responding to – all the emotions. Keep going until you are sure that all contradictory body-language signs have gone and only consistent signals remain.

Keeping Control

Some emotional reactions – like a squeal of delight from a two-year-old or a scream of shock from a twelve-year-old – are simply uncontrollable. But many emotional reactions are manageable, and we expect children to be able to control them. Exactly how much emotional control is expected is often determined by gender: boys are allowed more anger and girls more tears. It can also be influenced by culture: Japanese children are expected to hide upsetting feelings completely behind a smile at an age when most Western children are still being allowed to cry. And it is certainly determined by age: we largely accept the seventy per cent of toddlers who have temper tantrums, while by twelve years of age, as one questionnaire respondent put it, 'sitting and talking expressively takes the heat out of the situation'.

To what extent can a child – or adult – control emotions? We are certainly in charge of our gestures and movements; we can largely influence our facial expressions, overlaying an unacceptable feeling, such as anger, with an acceptable expression, like a smile. What we cannot control, though, is what goes on inside; unless trained in biofeedback, we have no way of regulating our heartbeat, blood pressure or adrenalin flow, which will continue to signal panic or attack whatever our external appearance. And in fact, studies have shown that people who suppress their external signs of emotion develop a stronger internal response from their nervous systems. By trying to keep calm, we increase the likelihood of feeling stressed.

If, then, a child feels an emotion (or an incongruent mix of one or more emotions), yet knows that she must not express it and so attempts to suppress her

---

THE SIGNS OF SUPPRESSED AND OVERWHELMING EMOTION

Whether playing emotion down or allowing it to well up, a child shows clear signs of needing help when emotion is not expressed in a balanced way. See below for examples of both.

	SUPPRESSED EMOTION	OVERWHELMING EMOTION
Why?	Child trying to 'be good' when aware of the dangers of showing emotion	Child is naturally strongly emotional, going through a toddler-tantrum phase or having a panic attack; tries to suppress emotion and fails
Example	Karen, ten, a normally 'good' child, upset about holiday plans, but wary of saying so during a family discussion	Suzie, thirteen, feels pulled between the demands of her parents for her to stay at home, and those of her friends for her to go out; she feels anger and rising panic when pressurized
What do you see?	Karen becomes very still; leans inwards; her facial expression turns 'blank' but shows tiny signs of anger and tears; she loses eye contact; fidgets or fiddles with quick, violent movements that show her suppressed anger; does not want to talk or be touched in case she lets out her real feelings	Suzie suddenly 'cracks'; her movements are strong and uncontrollable, exaggerated and repeated; her facial expression is contorted, with staring eyes and tears; she breathes quickly, her colour heightens, her heartrate rises; she shows no response when Mum tries to calm her
What do you hear?	Very little; Karen does not dare say what she wants to; when she does speak, her voice is flat and unemotional	Words and sounds at high volume; repeated phrases such as 'I don't know', 'Don't tell me what to do'; stumbles over words
What does the child experience?	Internal picture of holiday, which feels bad; internal voice telling her not to speak; heavy, anaesthetized, no sensation as she blocks off her feelings even to herself	Internal picture of disco she wants to go to; internal sound of friends' voices saying 'You should have come'; lots of sensation pulling her one way then another – 'fizzing', 'rushing', 'hot and cold' – all of it uncomfortable

feelings, her body will create stronger and stronger internal signals in order to get attention. The child's response to all this may be to suppress the emotion even further. She may succeed in doing this all the time and end up as a kinaesthetically blocked adult. She may, on the other hand, be able to suppress her feelings only so far; her increasingly strong internal signals will overwhelm her and the result is an out-pouring of violent emotion, which panics not only you but her as well.

The problem with total emotional expression is that it is against society. Nobody wants a child who manifests every emotion she feels every time she feels it. The problem with total emotional suppression is that it is against instinct. If a child's nervous system response is not expressed in action, then the jolt of preparatory activity a child's body has received remains unused. If this happens time after time, the child may develop stress symptoms, illness or depression. This book is not designed to offer solutions to deep-level problems that require in-depth counselling; for the child who occasionally pushes down what she feels or sometimes goes over the top and lets everything show, however, some suggestions follow.

Coping with Crisis

If your child seems to be feeling emotion but not expressing it, you will already have noticed this from the micromovements of emotion that are leaking out or from her overcontrolled posture. Such body language is most likely in an older child and may reach a crisis point in adolescence.

The main solution is to convince the child that being open will not cause havoc. When telling her this, you also need to give the same non-verbal message through movement, friendly expression and gentle voice tone. Most importantly, be prepared for when the emotions do come out. If the child is frightened of expressing them, the chances are that those emotions will be negative ones, but you still need to maintain accepting, safe body language.

What if the child's emotional suppression is more

Emotion often overwhelms in stages. A child's extremities may first signal trouble, clutching at clothing, toys or you. Next, the face will crumple, often seeming at odds with the body, which can appear slumped or calm. The final step will be an amplification of appeal signals through larger, more noticeable body signs.

CRISIS MANAGEMENT

Once your child is old enough to want to control emotion, she is old enough to do so. Cathartic therapies which encourage the expression of strong emotion, have over the past thirty years also developed ways to control it. These body-language strategies can be taught before an attack, then used as soon as the child spots the very first signals. If she learns that she can survive an emotional attack, she will be less frightened of it happening again.

Get the child to
- Change her position immediately to a more upright one.
- Get on her feet and move around.
- Keep her head up and eyes focused above the eye line.
- Do some kind of complex but non-risky physical activity that engages her attention, such as wiggling her fingers an increasing number of times.
- Do some kind of complex but undemanding mental activity that engages her attention, such as counting all the flowers on the wallpaper.
- Breathe deeply and slowly.

deep-rooted, and verbal encouragement to 'come clean' is not enough? She may literally withdraw from any interaction that threatens to bring her kinaesthetic channel back into play and increase the danger of emotion overwhelming her; so she will not accept touch. An effective, though demanding, alternative is constant matching (*see page 36*) – copying in a very general and supportive way her posture, gestures, expressions, voice tone and even breathing patterns – to reassure the child through her visual and auditory sensory channels that you are on her side. These, the basics of bonding, can magically re-establish a deep and trusting relationship.

If your child really has withdrawn from you, however, you may need to keep going for several days, accurately matching your child whenever you and she are together, before you regain enough rapport for the child to respond. You may find that the exercise of matching your child constantly will not only make her feel closer to you; it will also make you feel closer to her and so may remove the cause of the problem altogether. If not, when she does start to allow the emotion to show, the raw voice of grief, the

shaking of fear or the violence of anger may be so strong that they seem overwhelming.

How should you respond to a child whose feelings overpower her? If emotion overwhelms, with violent or rocking movements, shouts or screams, use as your basis all the basic techniques outlined earlier on page 48. With a temper tantrum, stay in the room and close but not touching, making sure that the child harms neither herself nor you. For panic or grief attacks, expect the child to regress in her body language; approach and touch, using comforting techniques that worked when she was younger.

If a child seems so out of control that the behaviour becomes frightening to you or her, move her attention away from her internal body signals, which are so strong that she cannot cope with them. Look into her eyes – move, bend or lie down if you have to – and do not worry if she stares straight through you. Then repeat her name softly, pausing each time you say it, rising in volume until you notice a gradual shift of eye focus or facial expression that tells you she is responding. Keep saying her name calmly and gradually begin to touch her.

Matthew's position supports him (top left) through body contact with something solid and also allows him to withdraw from contact and turn his attention inwards. Emotional words kept in by the child (top right) who is suppressing are indicated by biting lower lip, lips pressed together, hand over mouth, hand to throat or chest. Ask 'What do you really want to say?' then listen to the answer. Weariness occurs when energy is used to push emotion down (bottom left). This is a key sign of suppression, when combined with a face-hiding gesture.

TO21888

CHAPTER FOUR

PERSONALITY

Up to now, the body language I have explored has been transient. An expression comes and goes, a movement occurs and is over. This chapter looks at more long-lasting patterns of non-verbal behaviour, the ones that show an underlying aspect of your child's life – his personality.

Body language, more than anything else, will reveal your child's character. His words may explain what he means but his body language says who he is. And a child's body language not only demonstrates his personality, it also creates it. When people see a child's non-verbal communication they will react to him in a certain way. That, in turn, will influence the way in which he sees himself and so have an effect on his personality, which will affect his body language.

The first element to focus on is basic appearance. Your child's fundamental body-language inheritance comes in a package predetermined from conception.

gender, potential height, weight, colouring, face shape. The illustration and caption below outline some of the elements of appearance that matter, and explain why they do.

You may feel concerned. It can sometimes seem as if only tall, mature-faced, normal-looking children with perfect eyesight have any chance of succeeding in the world. But be reassured. Studies of adults have shown that, although first impressions are important, impression is only partly created by physical appearance. If your child's non-verbal behaviour – movement, gesture, eye contact – creates a good feeling in others, after a very short time his physical appearance becomes unimportant.

Personality Patterns

Your child will, over time, also develop patterns of body language that manifest her personality. Take, for example, extroversion and introversion. These terms refer to a character spectrum ranging from very internally-focused to very outgoing, and is currently one of the most widely recognized personality distinctions. An extrovert child may not be any more socially competent than an introvert but she will feel comfortable in large groups and find it easy to get on with new people.

How does body language reveal whether your child is an extrovert or an introvert? Take two sisters:

ATTRACTIVENESS ATTRACTS

We respond more positively to 'pretty' or 'handsome' children, judging what they do and say to be more intelligent and effective.

Judith Langlois specializes in studying human views of attractiveness. Her work suggests these views are innate. In a 1987 experiment, children as young as two and three-month-old babies looked much longer at a face seen by adults as attractive. In a 1990 study, Langlois showed that these 'attractive faces' approximate a mathematical average of all faces in a particular population. Good-looking means normal.

Furthermore, when we behave differently to a child because of attractiveness, we create differences in his self-image. Langlois's work, among others, shows that attractive children do indeed get better grades at school. Behaviour, however, compensates. Whether attractive or not, the child competent at body language will succeed.

Gender: girls better-behaved, boys allowed to talk more. Height: taller children treated like adults, smaller children are babied. Weight: underweight children get more attention, overweight ones are more unpopular. Skin colour: norm is seen as acceptable, the unusual viewed with suspicion. Face: a baby-faced child seems less intelligent, a mature-faced one more so. Eyes: a 1974 study suggests dark-eyed people have quicker reactions, light-eyed people think ahead. Glasses: children seen as swots may be bullied. Birth marks or handicaps: attract negative attention. Smell: an odd smell may lead to ostracism.

Juliet, an eight-year-old extrovert, and Tamara, a ten-year-old introvert. In groups, Juliet's posture, gestures and movements are easy and relaxed. Her voice is high and clear, her colour good. She feels energetic and invigorated. She shows no tension, no 'escape' movements of feet or hands unless she is tired and needs peace and quiet. She will move in close, cuddle up, look at other people, be happy when they look at her. Once over the 'stranger fear' of infancy, she has always been quite happy meeting new people for the first time – smiling, talking, listening and asking questions.

Already, even quite early in childhood, Juliet's face reveals the tiny upward diagonal lines at the corners of her mouth that show she smiles a lot. She permanently shows many of the signs that indicate open attention channels, such as wide eyes and pricked up ears. Because her channels are so open so often, her body 'sets' itself in these patterns, displaying small signs of them even when she is not paying attention to anything.

Tamara is very different. She hates being in groups. If she is not with people she knows well, she would

Extrovert versus introvert. The girls in the centre of the group react naturally to the photographer, face the camera, smile and keep eye contact. At each end of the group, two natural introverts keep their emotional distance, turning away, shielding themselves from view with hat and glasses. Their hunched shoulders and pouted mouths signal 'keep off'.

rather play alone. If she does find herself in a crowd, her body language immediately changes. She feels her stomach trembling and her mouth dry. Her eyes drop, her body stiffens. She even unconsciously tenses the muscles in her neck, making it difficult for her to turn easily to other children and make contact with them. She will take a long while to get used to strangers, and when forced to be with people she does not like will turn pale, go into constant downtime, or give tiny 'escape movements' of feet, shoulders, head. And already she looks 'unfriendly', with slightly hunched shoulders and a frown, a permanent expression that tends to deter people from approaching her. Her body, like Juliet's, has become set in a particular pattern.

Inherited or Learned?

n body-language terms there are many suggested explanations of the sisters' behaviour. One fascinating physiological hypothesis suggests that extrovert Juliet's nervous system may be less easily aroused than Tamara's, meaning that in order to get the same level of stimulation from being with other people, she has to make more contact: eye contact, voice contact and body contact. Introvert Tamara, on the other hand, may have a more easily excitable nervous system. To avoid being overloaded with human contact – the most stimulating contact that children can have – she unconsciously sets up body language barriers. If she does not, her body complains.

Secondly, it is highly likely that many of these personality differences can be explained by the non-verbal behaviour each little girl has developed as a response to her general life experience. Tamara, as a first child, may have got used to playing alone, and her body now gives off deterrent signals to keep her protected from others (*see page 73*). Juliet, on the other hand, growing up with a sister in the house, may like company; her body-language signals encourage other people to approach.

And thirdly, the two girls may have modelled non-verbal cues from people important to them. As Tamara was growing up as a first baby, perhaps her nervous parents gave inconsistent body-language signs in response to her developing social skills so that she was left feeling unsure and distressed about how to respond to other people non-verbally. By the time Juliet came along, the parents had been able to give more encouraging non-verbal feedback to her early signs of interaction, with the result that she now enters social situations with a good feeling inside and a positive internal dialogue.

Whatever the cause of children's body language, the effects will be the same. Repeated day-to-day use of any particular set of non-verbal signals will etch itself onto their physical appearance, at a remarkably early age. These are outward signs to the world that a child thinks or feels in a particular way; they are clear statements of that child's approach to life.

Now that you have grasped some essentials of the body language of personality, you may want to be aware of any generalized patterns of body language that your child manifests; not occasional emotional responses or contextualized reactions, but consistent postures, repeated movement patterns and permanent facial expressions. They may indicate extroversion or introversion or other established personality traits. What do these non-verbal 'personality patterns' say to you about your child's character?

IS SHAPE THE KEY TO PERSONALITY?

There may be no link between a child's body shape and her 'real' personality, but there certainly is a correlation between shape and how we react to it. An American study showed that students with the three classic body shapes (defined as endomorphic, ectomorphic and mesomorphic, by William Sheldon in the 1940s) were responded to by teachers in the ways shown in the chart.

	ENDOMORPH	ECTOMORPH	MESOMORPH
Shape of child's body	Oval with large abdomen	Fragile, not muscular; flatchested if a girl	Muscular, broad-shouldered, firm
How the child is seen	If a girl, 'curvy'; if a boy, 'podgy'	If a girl, boyish and attractive; if a boy, 'swotty'	Physically attractive, 'the right shape'
Perceived fitness	Unfit	Fit, but not an athlete	Fit, athletic, strong
Perceived intelligence	Slow, lazy, unintelligent	Intelligent and competent	Bright but not intellectual
Perceived temperament	Relaxed, at ease	Nervous and anxious	Enterprising, confident, mature
Perceived sociability	Friendly, funny, warm-hearted	Highly strung, difficult, unfriendly	Dominant, socially effective

Personality Changes

Most children's personality patterns are a joy to themselves and their families. Some, however, may seem to be a problem. In many of the other sections of the book, I have suggested non-verbal solutions for 'problems' that appear only temporarily or in one context, such as a lack of confidence, or an inability to spell. Here, however, the issue is consistent patterns of behaviour that often have existed from birth, such as a child who is 'naturally' optimistic or pessimistic; stubborn or biddable; confident or timid. So is there anything body language can do to change them?

Firstly, ask yourself if change is really necessary. As you are more sensitive to your child's behaviour than anyone else, it is possible that a pattern of body language with which you are unhappy does not create a problem for other people. Your irresponsible child may seem to other adults to be delightfully carefree; your over-serious child may impress her teachers as a dedicated student. So relax. Your non-verbal communication of tension about the way your child's character is developing is probably doing more to create the problem than any other factor.

One personality theory divides people according to what attracts their attention and motivates them. Achievers are most interested in how they can succeed in life. Affiliators (below) are naturally drawn towards others – notice the eye contact and body touching. Power-sorters (far right) look for the dominance possibilities in any situation.

If, however, you do feel that your child's long-term approach to life needs changing, then this may be one of those occasions when body-language solutions are just not enough. Deep-rooted change often requires talk-based counselling. And it may not be your child who needs that help. Challenging though you may find the suggestion, do check out whether someone in your family is the model for the very body language that forms the basis of your child's personality. Studies show, for example, that most depressive children come from a family with one depressive parent, and that the children pick up that condition more through body-language signals than through the parent confiding in the child verbally. If this scenario strikes a chord in you, please consider counselling for yourself or other relevant family members (*see Contact Organizations, page 125*). If your family gets support, I promise that it will help your child to be more happy and successful.

Personality Solutions

What if the problem is not serious yet cannot be ignored? You love your child, he is basically fine, but you want his fundamental body language to change. You want your mildly introverted seven-year-old to make more friends; or you long for your placator son to start standing up for himself. How can you get a child to shift his personality patterns long-term?

There are ways. Whatever your child's constitutional personality, giving him more effective 'temporary' body language – appearance changes, gesture, movement, eye-contact patterns – will work for three reasons. Firstly, a change on the outside can often encourage the body to feel differently on the inside. Secondly an outside shift will alter the way others treat the child and so help him behave differently. Thirdly, if a child constantly uses the new body language, it may well, in time, take root and become more 'real' than the original.

If, for example, aspects of your child's basic physique have the potential to create bias in the people he meets, you can compensate. I am not suggesting over-priced 'cosmetic' solutions, but sensible ways to tip the balance. Encourage your overweight child to get fit and develop a healthy shape. Be sympathetic to pleas for flattering glasses or contact lenses, not embarrassing equivalents and offer make-up lessons to hide a birthmark. Consider shifting your own approach to your child's appearance. Invest money and time into getting him a good

haircut and well-cut clothes to be worn at school as well as at home. This seems a totally surface solution, but if your child's approach to life is to under-achieve, this answer may just work. Keep up the effort: give him a successful outer shell for at least a year from now and his whole body language will shift.

Next, consider giving your child regular rehearsals in the 'body language of euphoria' – exercise. Studies have shown that one of the most successful ways to help people feel dramatically more optimistic about life in general and themselves in particular is to get them moving. Does your child play sport? If not, would he dance? What about one of the gentle posture-improvement methods such as Alexander Technique, or a movement-based support system such as drama therapy?

You can also give specific coaching on the skills your child may be lacking. Even if the theories are true that personality is created by genetically inherited body traits, skills can help. Your child will, for example, benefit from learning basic social competence (*see page 68*). Teaching him the rules of social interaction will allow him to feel more in control and less threatened. In the same way, many seemingly immovable personality traits such as general unhappiness, wimpishness or nervousness can be helped long-term by regular use of the exercises I suggest on confidence-building (*see page 97*), persuasion-resistance (*see page 71*) or emotion-calming (*see page 53*).

A final and not altogether tongue-in-cheek solution to your problem-personality child is this. Try waiting until the next major turning point in his life, such as starting school or reaching puberty. These turning points can create real shifts. The vast alterations to self-esteem and social competence that happen when a previously tyrannical rising-three goes to play school have to be seen to be believed. And the changes to appearance and hormones that occur when a child reaches sexual maturity can turn a sullen monster into an utterly charming young man.

Therapist Virginia Satir identified four non-verbal patterns that children use when under threat. The blamer (top) feels bad about herself and others; stiff posture, tense neck and throat, hard, tight voice, tight breath. The placator (middle) tries to please; strained posture, upwards gaze, tentative voice, hand to mouth to stop the words. The computer (bottom) analyzes rather than feels; rigid spine, averted gaze, unvaried voice. The fourth pattern, distractor, combines the other three with shifting movement and voice tone.

ONE TO ONE

A child's first and most important relationship is with the key adult or adults in his life. And that relationship is vital. A new-born's body is programmed to demand an adult's attention to make sure he gets his physical needs met: that he is fed, kept warm, and protected. His body needs not only to feel full, warm and dry but also to have regular touch, the sight and sound of another person and the right smell next to it. Take away this 'bond' and the baby's body simply cannot function properly. New-borns, even if well cared for physically, become ill if they do not get enough human contact. Equally, the baby who does not 'bond', and so gets no early models to learn from, does not pick up the right non-verbal signs. He simply does not get a chance to learn to be happily human.

Bonding is not about a baby actively attaching itself to a passing adult. A new-born does not have that much chance or choice. What the baby has to do is to persuade the relevant adult to bond to it, thereby guaranteeing full-time loving care for at least several years. How does the baby manage it?

The process largely happens through non-verbal communication, which begins in the womb, then

All the elements of bonding are seen clearly here. Eye contact and a broad smile draw Mum to baby and make sure baby learns what it is to be human from Mum. By a few months old, baby's instinct to match and his delight in seeing Mum do the same has developed into a bonding force for both of them.

THE STEPS TO BONDING

How does bonding first happen and then develop? This chart focuses on how the three major senses *account for the majority of your child's bonding experiences through childhood.*

	BEFORE BIRTH	AFTER BIRTH	PRE-VERBAL CHILDHOOD	POST-VERBAL CHILDHOOD
How important is bonding?	Vital; up to birth, baby will die unless bond with mother is maintained	Without it, baby can survive, but may fail to develop normally	Still vital for emotional development. By seven months, main bond has been formed with key carers	Increasingly less important; by adolescence, the bond must loosen to enable maturing
Through sound	Heartbeat and pulse rhythm of mother and baby synchronize in the womb, adding to the bonding	Carer's voice replaces heartbeat. Baby's cry is programmed to bond him to the carer, while carer often uses a special tone of voice for talking only to baby	Crying is still a main bonding tool, but 'babbling' lets carer and child communicate at a distance	Unique human speech skills maintain bonds from far away
Through touch	Months of precise 'motion tracking' put mother and baby in an almost trance-like state of bonding	Continuous touch reduces alarmingly at birth. Being held and suckling – which give touch, smell and taste – reward both carer and baby	Clinging reflexes in hands and arms – part of monkey inheritance – remain for two months. Holding on is a main source of bonding well into childhood	Drops dramatically to a fraction of what it was at birth and is more formal
Through sight		Baby now sees carer; her dilated pupils say 'I like you', creating an instinctive emotional bonding response	Eye contact continues to bond. Smiles begin. Unique to humans, they reward and reassure both carer and child	Eye contact and smiles continue through childhood, but may drop off in adolescence when a child wants more independence: the 'she never looks at me' syndrome

develops through different sensory channels over time. Throughout this process the baby's appearance and body language not only attract the adult, but at the same time give an incredibly high degree of reward in order to keep the adult motivated to stay and to care during this stage.

The first few days and weeks after a baby is born are significant for bonding. Although the mother is the favourite target, the baby can bond with any appropriate adult at this time. This is a neat precaution built in by nature just in case the mother has died in childbirth. After several months the baby starts to suffer from stranger anxiety; he reserves his best attention – eye contact, smiles, speech-like gurgles – for those most likely to be permanent fixtures in his life, the people who care for him, thus bonding them to him even more firmly.

A Closer Bond

Do not panic if you have not had full access to your child during this early period. You may have missed out on a delightful experience but it does not mean you cannot bond. A study by psychologists Hatch and Maietta in New Mexico suggests that adults can rebond to children at any time by reproducing what happens in the womb. They claim the main human bonding activity is 'motion tracking', a complex and

A BABY'S MOST POWERFUL TOOL

A baby's appearance is genetically programmed to make absolutely sure that she is cared for. It creates in others an overpowering urge to touch, nurture and smile at her. In his book *Babywatching*, Desmond Morris describes experiments carried out to find out what the crucial aspects of a baby's appearance are. In one, adults watched a series of pictures; their response was measured through their pupil dilation, a sign of interest and approval that is not consciously controlled. Results showed that these elements are vital:

- A large head in comparison with body.
- A prominent, bulbous forehead.
- Large eyes, pale in colour to show clearly any pupil dilation.
- Rounded, protruding cheeks.
- Small size.
- Short, heavy limbs.
- Plump, rounded body.

deep-level form of matching that happens during pregnancy. Beginning with fertilization and cell division and continuing right through to labour, it involves mother and baby in leading and following each other's movements.

After birth, it is matching in gesture and movement that forms the main unconscious bonding mechanism between child and adult. Further, Hatch and Maietta say that matching can be consciously used as a bonding mechanism to build your adult-child relationship continually, or even to re-establish it if there has been some sort of breakdown. Matching is also, not surprisingly, an important element of rapport between two friends, children or adults.

To practise matching with your baby, start from the way she is moving and let her lead you, rather than

As well as bonding, a child can de-bond. If one child is preferred, or simply gets on better with his parents than another does, then the less popular child may show de-bonding signs – lack of eye contact, an unwillingness to get involved, mismatching of expression or movement and a reluctance to touch.

imposing your movement on her. One mother reports, 'When Jilly was just a few weeks' old, I touched her fingers and followed her speed, direction and timing. I followed her, but then, quite quickly, she started to follow me – with a gurgle of glee then reversing the process. We still play this game; she is five now.'

With a child young enough to want to play movement games, try 'mirroring', with you as one side of the mirror and the child as the other. With an older child you may have to settle for matching at a distance to allow you the chance to rebond at a physical level. Try walking together and matching pace, speed and body posture; swimming together side-by-side; dancing and matching to the music; or even going on a fairground ride together and simultaneously holding tight on the hair-raising bits. The trick is not to slavishly or exaggeratedly imitate, which can seem mocking, but to respectfully 'take on' the child's movements as closely as possible, and then respond instinctively as first one then the other of you takes the lead.

Breaking Away

Bonding is essential, but children need to break the bond if they are to survive later as independent adults. Monkey groups, which offer total physical support and protection to their babies when young, end up punishing young monkeys if they try to cling on after a certain age. Human parents do not do quite that, but they do encourage the natural ebb of bonding body language as a child gets older.

Bonding body language may first start to ebb at around the time a toddler learns to talk, or perhaps just after he goes to school. At five, Philip suddenly did not like touch, would not kiss goodbye, refused bedtime snuggles. He looked at everything or everyone except Mum, and did not smile at her in the same way he used to. The effect of this kind of behaviour can be devastating but what was happening was, in fact, totally natural. At this point in his life a child can bond at a distance through words. The more overt bonding signs can therefore disappear, although they usually reappear in a very short while just to make

A young monkey hangs onto its parent's long fur as the adult swings through the jungle. In the absence of fur, Laura, like many young children when unhappy, hangs on to her Mum's leg and comforts herself with face and body pressed close. Mum, meanwhile, adds to the comfort with a supporting hand on Laura's back.

sure that you are still available. The child will then settle down to another few years of being cuddly and smiley once again.

How should you handle this stage? Calmly. Tell yourself and your child that this is to be expected, and try not to insist on the former level of snuggles and cuddles. If your body-language message is that it is fine to move away, your child will soon come back.

Clinging On

At some point between the ages of five and eleven comes a total reversal of the aforementioned break for independence. A child may become terrified of abandonment, internally making pictures of a world without you. Jan, aged seven 'has, over the last few days, discovered he wants to spend every minute with me . . .'. Your child may be less naughty, more biddable, may use illness as an excuse for attention. He may regress to positions or gestures he used when little, like thumb-sucking.

His body is reacting to possible abandonment in exactly the same way as it did when he was two weeks old. Inside he gets panic messages; outside, he clings. If he is young, play 'matching' games with him to reassure; or reintroduce 'peek-a-boo' games which, even before he could talk, taught him that people can both go away and come back again. Whatever age he is, spend some 'quiet time' with him each day, not necessarily playing or even talking, but showing him through your companionable body language that you are not going to leave. Give as much touch and physical reassurance as you can, and whenever there is a separation make sure that the child carries with him some sort of reminder of your presence. Suit it to his favourite sensory channel: a photo of you or a personal stereo with family voices on tape.

The next crisis will be at adolescence. Your child will naturally be spending more time away from home, gaining his independence through choosing his own clothes, music and company. So why does he also need to cut you off with his body language? No eye contact, no smiles, no sign of matching, and definitely no touching, even if this same child, just a year ago, hugged and kissed you every time he left the house. His posture becomes still and withdrawn, his voice goes flat when he speaks to you; once on the phone to friends, though, the tone will become animated again.

If a young person feels, albeit unconsciously, that the bond he has with you is beginning to challenge his independence, then body language will insert a fire-break between you. As with a toddler, your adolescent will need to come back for reassurance; so with Dad he may opt for touch in the form of rough-and-tumble, while with Mum he may mysteriously get ill or hang around silently for attention. Again, like the toddler, what he really needs is an open door when he wants it, and for you not to be alarmed by his body language. Given time, once he is sure that it is safe to rebond, he will be back.

Making Contact

From the very start of her life your child has the intrinsic skills needed to form human relationships. As well as all the gazing, touching, smiling and matching capabilities of bonding that have already been mentioned, she has other, equally important, talents. Within just a few minutes of birth, she will naturally prefer looking at faces to anything else. She can show her intense interest in another person through widening her eyes, opening her mouth, leaning her body forward, reaching out her arms and hands and pointing her fingers and toes, hanging on tight and snuggling closer. The natural rhythm of her life, which has active times and quiet times, has made her aware that relationships have periods of activity and of non-activity. As a result, very shortly after birth she has mastered the basics of relationship turn-taking, being at ease with a 'you do something, then I will do something' mode of interaction. All these signals, originally aimed at survival, form the basis of social competence, which we call 'rapport'.

As she grows, your child will naturally maintain and develop these skills. One questionnaire respondent said that her little girl of two-and-a-half 'looks into her friend's eyes and copies her expressions and actions'. If, on the other hand, your child feels uneasy, she will naturally contradict rapport signs by moving away, losing eye contact, even crying if she has to hug someone she does not like. Your child may learn to hide signs of dislike as she gets older, and give a 'social smile', one that involves the mouth only and not the muscles around the eyes, which cannot be consciously controlled. Because children are less skilled at hiding their real feelings, however, you may be able to spot the micromovements of dislike in eyes or mouth. Interestingly, though, many of the intrinsic relationship abilities that a child has at birth become less effective as she gets older. Eye gaze and smiles, for example, may be lost if a child learns to be shy or

LEARNING SOCIAL COMPETENCE

Children seem to pick up the 'rules of rapport' naturally but only as they grow. You can help speed up the process.

● Teach your child the rules. Stand near but not too near; lean forwards slightly; look at the person's eyes, not around the room; do not fidget; give approval signs such as smiles and nods. (More detailed rules for conversation are explained on page 72.)
● Integrate all this by getting the child to notice how she likes others to treat her. Ask specific questions, such as 'What does she do that makes you want to play with her? . . . What happened to make you dislike her?' A younger child will answer in vague terms: a friend was nice, the adult was horrid. An older child will be able to identify just what it was that made the difference: her friend looked at her, the adult hugged her without permission.
● Get the child to notice how others respond to her attempts at rapport. 'Did he like your doing that? . . . How do you know? . . . What did she do when you did that?' Signs that a child is not getting rapport might include the other person moving back, looking away, frowning. When that is reported, ask 'What do you think you could have done to make that person feel better?'
● You will be surprised how instinctively, at that point, most children will reply 'I could have smiled at her . . . I think I was standing too close.'
● Reward all attempts at rapport, even if you privately think they will not work, as long as your child is able to judge their effectiveness. As always, you are teaching an approach rather than a set of rules.

needs downtime. By the time they reach eight or nine, boys in particular can have great difficulty showing normal rapport signals, particularly in emotional situations. I once watched a rugby cup final where the adult players, triumphantly coming up to get their medals, looked the medal-presenting officials full in the eye and gave beaming grins. Yet three hours earlier, in the preceding youth match, their twelve-year-old counterparts had, to a man, all received their medals with serious and averted gaze, leaving the row of presenting officials bemused.

Many of the rapport signs a child uses make adults uneasy. A child who comes too close may make the

Children often don't realize the effect their body language has on adults who work by the 'rules of rapport'. The lad's crossed arms and slight pout (above), as well as his 'doing nothing' air, provoke immediate irritation in his father. There is a lack of interaction, as the boy's defocused gaze and blank, withdrawn expression leaves the father with no way in. By failing to make eye contact, speak, or reach out to touch, the boy (left) leaves the adult wondering whether he wants to interact or not, and unsure how to respond.

older person feel invaded. Most adults are comfortable with a 'personal' distance of 0.5 to 1.2 metres ($1\frac{1}{2}$ to 4 feet). This feeling of invasion, interestingly, heightens the older the child is. Perhaps this is a throw-back to the monkey unwillingness to support older offspring.

A final problem is that many of the formalized signs used by adults are not ones that children know instinctively; they are learned over time. The nods, smiles and expressions of agreement that adults use in Western society, for example, are not fully mastered by children until pre-adolescence which may lead an adult into believing that a child is bored or not listening. Equally, rapport signs differ from culture to culture; the close proximity and full eye contact of Afro-Caribbean cultures may be interpreted as rudeness or forwardness by members of other cultures. The panel on page 68 gives you some hints for helping your child to learn rapport rules as she grows.

Making Friends

What happens when your child makes friends? His body is then instinctively fulfilling two non-verbal functions. Firstly, it alerts other people to a particular relationship that they should treat with care. 'Hands off, we have a special connection' says the body language. Two friends will often display obvious and very formal signs of attachment called 'tie signs': linked arms or hand-holding, a hug or kiss on greeting, identical clothes or badges. When together, they may also set up actual barriers – perhaps with toys or their own spread-eagled bodies – blocking off their own personal space, clearly indicating that they are not available to other people.

Secondly, the body language of special friendship actually works to maintain the relationship. Each child is signalling to the other, in very much the same way as they did to their parents when they were babies, the bonding messages 'I like you . . . You are attractive to me . . . Please stay'. The way in which this begins, and the initial trigger that sparks the attraction, varies with each relationship. Once in place, however, all the signs of 'rapport' that are usually brought into play to signal a general interest in people move to their ultimate extreme. A child's increasing closeness, his smiles, the pupil dilation of his eyes all validate the other child on a totally unconscious level. In return, he receives equal non-verbal messages of appreciation.

The result is a mutual admiration society and strongly stimulating effect on both children's external and physical function signs. They will react to each other in all the 'positive attention' ways outlined in Chapter One. They will be markedly physiologically more excited to see each other than they are to meet other people. Oliver, aged two, 'will stand in front of his special friend laughing and jumping up and down. He smiles as soon as he sees her'. Their heartbeat may rise with exhilaration; they will literally have more energy, for younger children to use in movement and playing, for older children to use in talking, thinking and swapping stories. The stimulation attracts the children to each other even more in a continuing spiral of good feeling.

As the relationship develops, so rapport deepens. Friends will be more relaxed and informal with each other than with other children because they feel safe. Long-term friends will not need a full range of responses in order to communicate. Simon, aged

ine, and his next-door neighbour often 'settle down
o play side-by-side. They do not look at each other
much, or even talk a lot. But when they play, they
eem to know instinctively what moves the other is
making, passing toys across without even looking.
hey also squabble quite happily, and never seem to
eed to make up'.

Signs of Trouble

What happens when a friendship goes wrong? A
oddler's friendship problems will develop, come to a
head and be resolved within a very short time-span. If

*Friendship body language differs with gender. Girls
need closeness, more touching, talking, eye contact and
matching. Boys' friendships are active and competitive,
with more status displays, movement and flashes of
aggression. This may be due to their nervous systems
needing different kinds and amounts of input.*

another child upsets him, he will react immediately
and directly. One little boy of two and a half,
described in the questionnaire, was typical: 'He will
push friends away when they have done something to
upset him. His body will become tense. He may resort
to biting in extreme frustration.' The problem here is
that, after the extreme reassurance of friendship signs
such as matching, the sudden abandonment when a
friend loses interest is devastating to a little one. The
physiological functions react swiftly. All you can do is
offer comfort in the ways described on page 48.

Past toddlerhood, longer-term friendships can be
formed; their breakdown can be both more subtle

THE ART OF PERSUASION-RESISTANCE

Children's skill in persuading friends to do what
they want puts most advertising campaigns to
shame. Whether the issue is playing with a
forbidden toy, lending money or staying out late,
you may well want to equip your child to resist
peer pressure. A verbal 'no', however, may not be
enough, unless it is backed up by non-verbal
resistance.

A child who persuades successfully
● Moves close.
● Holds eye contact to the point that it becomes
  uncomfortable for the receiver.
● Smiles slightly when the 'victim' is weakening,
  frowns slightly when the victim resists.
● Looks rejected when the answer is no: slumps,
  looks down, turns away, lets voice get low and
  slow; or looks threatening: stands very close,
  jabs or points with finger, repeats request in an
  angry voice.

A child who resists persuasion successfully
● Knows about all the persuasion tactics outlined
  above and spots them coming.
● Is quick to notice his own internal sense of
  'wrongness' at the persuasion – trembles of fear,
  rushes of anger.
● Steps back to 'get distance' while listening to the
  request.
● Keeps a balanced, relaxed position, standing
  directly facing the other child.
● When saying no, faces persuader directly, keeps
  eye contact, does not smile, keeps voice low and
  even.
● If emotionally pressured turns away but
  maintains relaxed, confident body language.

CONVERSATION RULES

The rules of conversation are so complex that even many adults do not know them. Help your child learn the rules by explaining them clearly and demonstrating them in conversation. In particular, reward the child when she uses them correctly by allowing her the time and opportunity to speak. When someone is talking:

● Show interest by eye contact and nod at regular intervals and important points.
● Wait for a turn-taking signal – a drop in tone, a sweeping hand gesture, a pause and glance at the listener – before speaking (or give one to let the other person speak).
● Signal you want to speak by half-opening your mouth, audibly breathing in, raising your hand fractionally.
● Interrupt without speaking by touch, catching the speaker's eye, making a sudden movement.
● Give signals of 'stop please, I am not interested' by looking away, speeding up the nodding, moving your lips as if to speak.
● End a conversation by pausing for longer when speaking, giving less and less eye contact, making a sudden shift in posture.

and more confusing. He may literally not spot when things are going wrong because his erstwhile friend cannot be open about loss of interest. Reading the non-verbal signs here can make the message clear. To help, there are certain questions that you can encourage your child to ask himself. Does the friend move away when your child moves towards him? Is there equal eye contact, equal head turning, equal leaning forward? Has the balance of the children's conversation changed so that, rather than taking turns, one is now doing all the talking, the other all the listening? Has the 'friend's' voice tone changed from varied to flat, showing that he is feeling less emotional stimulation than before? Is supportive touching or mock-fighting now avoided? Are postures or gestures negative: fidgeting or 'escape' movements of the feet? Are facial expressions negative: tiny movements of mockery or hostility?

Once these signs of waning friendship have been spotted, what can the child do? It is more straight-

These women signal by body lean-ins and direct eye contact that they don't want to be distracted. In the face of this, the boy breaks adult conventions by physically interrupting. The younger he is, the more acceptable his behaviour – the older, the more negative the reaction will be to his rulebreaking.

ON HER OWN

Being alone, for a child who desires it is fine, but can be very painful for the lonely child. Use this *chart to check whether your child is lonely – or simply alone.*

	A CHILD WHO WANTS TO BE ALONE	A LONELY CHILD
Example	Lucy, seven, is quite happy playing by herself with a toy truck, even though other children are nearby	Jacolyn, six-and-a-half, is new to the school. She is playing with toy building bricks near a group of classmates
Posture	Lucy is turned away from the others, bent over her truck, showing where her attention is	Jacolyn never quite turns away from the group
Matching	Sometimes spontaneously matches her friends, which shows her closeness to them, but rarely looks at them to check this out	Never spontaneously matches her classmates; sometimes consciously tries to move into similar positions, but always looks across at the others to check whether she is succeeding
Movement	Moves a great deal, interacting with her truck; her big movements show confidence	Moves very little; often stops what she is doing, showing nervousness and a need to be accepted
Expression	Concentrated; spontaneous eye wrinkles; the way she smiles and talks to herself shows she is stimulated by her own company	Solemn; if she talks to herself often gives an irritated shake of the head. She is not happy with her own company
Eye contact	Shows where her attention is by looking at the truck, only occasionally looking away to remember or imagine something	Stares into space or looks at the others. She looks far more than she plays. Her attention is directed out towards her classmates, not in towards herself

forward to broach the subject verbally but it is also difficult, particularly for an insecure eleven-year-old. He has two non-verbal choices. He can either amplify his friendship signals, renewing and increasing all the old behaviour of a special friend; or he can pull back by using, in return, all the withdrawal body signs listed above. If the waning friend is really uninterested, then either of these options will hasten the *coup de grâce.* If, however, he is mistaken and the friend is just 'going through a phase', then either option will speedily result in a reunion.

Spending Time Alone

What if your child is on her own? Is it because she wants to be, or not? As we learned in Chapter Two, the child who wants to take time out, either momentarily or for a long while, may physiologically have very good reasons for that. Perhaps her sensory channels are sated. After a whole day (or in the case of a new-born a whole minute) spent interacting, she may desperately need 'downtime', a chance to process her thoughts. She may equally, want to spend time fantasizing, imagining, mentally or physically exploring or creating; these activities are largely dependent on not having to interact with others. In both cases, her body may well signal this to her, maintaining tension, a headache, fuzzy eyes or discomfort in her stomach or back until she gets the time alone that she needs.

Her body will also signal to others her need to be alone. The whole aim is to reduce interaction and stimulation. New-borns have this skill; they can turn or arch their whole body away from you, whine, fuss or spit to get the solitude they need. In older children, the signs are more socially acceptable: turning their heads, breaking off eye contact, shrugging the shoulders almost as if blocking the ears. If spoken to, the child may reply with a flat voice, with no variation in pitch or tone. And the child may also temporarily look unfriendly, to deter others from making contact. She may look stern, or put on a blank face. She may tighten her lips or frown. She is not cross about anything in particular, and she is almost certainly unaware of how she appears, but her body knows that such behaviour is a very good way to ensure

Oliver (near right) is secure enough in his place in the group to be happy on his own even though the others are talking. His firmly turned back, combined with his relaxed posture and concentration on what he is doing shows that he is not lonely. Far right, however, is a different story. A child in a gender minority is often automatically left out of group play, through no fault of his own but simply because he's not 'one of the girls' – or boys! His hovering on the edge of the group shows that he wants to be part of it.

being left alone. Your best ploy is to trust her instincts and allow her the extended solitude she wants.

One step on from the child who occasionally needs solitary downtime is the loner. This is a child who, for one reason or another, prefers to be alone most of the time. She may be an introvert whose nervous system feels uncomfortable with the high level of input that interaction with people demands (*see page 57*). She may have learned to value the high-quality thinking opportunities that being alone gives her; many creative geniuses demonstrate classic loner behaviour. Or she may simply be going through a phase due to internal upheaval such as puberty, or external problems such as exams; she needs to spend the majority of her time in solitude to process and cope with the crisis.

As well as using the sort of body language described above, the loner will mark out a definite, permanent territory – perhaps her bedroom – where she can go and be undisturbed. She may lock her door or put up a series of 'go away' posters. Most children use body language from time to time to signal their need to be alone, but the loner may adopt such non-verbal communication constantly. Her

permanent body language will include signs such as raised shoulders, a constantly averted gaze and a hostile expression.

A loner child may be a cause for your concern. If the retreat is obviously a phase, particularly at adolescence, then relax and allow her body to get what it needs. If the retreat is permanent and progressive, it is often because of some emotional problem; you will need to use all your affection and support to help, and you may want to consider professional counselling (*see Contact Organizations, page 125*).

Unwillingly Alone

What about the child who is alone but does not want to be? The signs are easily spotted and similar in some ways to the body language of 'ending friendship' (*see page 72*). If, for whatever reason, your child is being excluded, look out for other children avoiding her; keeping their distance; not maintaining eye contact or seeming permanently distracted when talking to her; blocking her off from what they are doing with their bodies or toys; looking at her blankly, unsmiling. This

is often a vicious circle. To begin with, your child may have failed to engage with a group, perhaps because she does not know how to. She may not have had much practice in making contact with new people; this in itself may make her withdrawn. Research suggests that a significant reason for children not being included in group activities is that, quite simply, they do not spontaneously join in. If she is excluded, for whatever reason, then the child may, quite naturally, start to look distressed or irritated. Unfortunately, research also suggests that the second main reason that children are not included is that they show subtle, often unconscious signs of negativity, such as distress or irritation.

How can you help? For a toddler or a child who has just started school, simply give lots of opportunity to practise making friends in different situations, and cuddles and hugs if something goes wrong. An older child, hitting a popularity problem in the way even very sociable children do occasionally, can be taught a more formal 'modelling' strategy to make and maintain contact.

Begin by getting your child to remember a time when a newcomer appeared, maybe in a school class or at a party. Did the newcomer look approachable? If so, what were his or her body signs? These are usually an open posture, interested eyes, a friendly face. You could maybe contrast this with a newcomer who looked unfriendly. What body language was he or she using that put people off? Either with or without formal practice of what works, these realizations will help your child to identify positive signs and adopt positive behaviour.

Add to these insights direct instructions of how to make contact. The child needs to scan around the room to catch another's eye and offer a slight smile. If the glance and smile are answered, perhaps with a small affirming nod, that is the signal to move closer and start to talk. At this point rapport skills are vital: turning towards the other child; keeping attention focused firmly on him or her without distraction; smiling, nodding, leaning forward. In time, once the relationship is established, there will be more than enough room for disagreement and friendly fights. But the essential aim of the first few minutes of any contact is to give the other person the message that they are accepted, and there is no quicker and more direct way to do that than through body language.

CHAPTER SIX

MAKING GROUPS WORK

Whatever your child's basic body language, it will change when he is in a group. This is because your child will be in some ways a different person when he is with other people. He will tend to diminish some types of behaviour and exaggerate others, be what one questionnaire respondent described as 'school self . . . home self . . . youth-club self . . .'. In his family he may, not surprisingly, behave like a child. Outside his family he may behave a lot more like an adult, sometimes to your horror, sometimes to your delight.

The behaviour your child shows could be called a role. This is because, in any group, an individual may need to play a part in order to make things work. The eldest child may get landed with the role of 'Mum' or 'Dad', helping parents to look after the other children physically and emotionally. This happens when adults need extra help or are unable or unwilling to do the parenting. The youngest in the class may be regarded as the 'baby', always left out of games or treated like a fool. Other people react to him like that; their body language, in particular, defines him like that; and he responds like that, mainly non-verbally. He gets something from it: the attention, the feeling he belongs, the fact that he has a job to do. The result emerges as a whole set of body-language signs that constitute your child's role in his group. And because

most groups are completely unaware of what roles their members play, you cannot just ask what is happening. You have to look at the body language.

You need to identify your child's role in any group for two reasons: to find out whether your child is content, and to check whether the role is good for him. Maybe he is playing Dad but resents the constant demands on him. Perhaps, because he is treated and acts like a baby, this makes you unhappy.

Role-swapping

How can a child switch roles or step out of a role he is unhappy with? This often happens naturally. A 'baby' child grows up and one day gets treated, and behaves, like an adult. Perhaps new members join the group and your child is no longer the 'baby'. Or maybe the child changes group: he moves to a new class and is not the youngest pupil.

If such a solution seems unlikely, you can create alternatives with a child who knows about body language. What elements of his non-verbal communication are most obviously saying 'baby'? What can you and he do to change them to new ones?

A role is not behaviour intrinsic to your child's personality. He does not, for instance, act like a baby

One group role that girls can play is that of the tomboy (see chart, page 78). Here we see three such girls, not yet needing to cover female body signs such as breasts, and still able to move their limbs in ways that will be unacceptable in a few years' time.

A group showing a classic role allocation according to size. The larger central boy plays the clown, while the noticeably smaller boy on the far right of the group seems likely to be cast in the role of baby.

all the time, only when with a particular group of people, family, friends or school-mates. If he chooses to, then he can probably simply stop acting 'baby' even when with those friends.

He may need some help. Encourage him to try modelling: copying more appropriate body language and using it effectively. For the first few days, he will be 'acting', a good word to use when describing modelling to an older child. After that, the new body language may well take over.

First, get your 'baby' to watch out for other children – real, on screen or imaginary – who behave in a more grown-up way. Do not worry if the body language he finds to copy is caricatured, such as an ultra-sophisticated look or a macho walk; it will not look like that once he starts using it for real. You are providing him with an alternative non-verbal way to begin to think of himself that will start to eradicate the 'baby' body language. Get him to practise – copying posture, movement, gesture, expression, voice tone – while you look out for added unconscious proof that he is also modelling in his more-relaxed breathing pattern or healthier-looking skin tone. Then get the child to imagine joining his group and behaving in

this way. Finally, get him to promise to keep up the 'act' for at least the next five times he is with his group. It will take that long for him to forget to 'act' and really begin to manifest more grown-up body language. It will also take that amount of time for the group to adapt to his new behaviour and stop trying to treat him like a baby.

A final caution. As well as having many roles with his various groups of friends, your child also has a role within your family. But is it a role the child wants to play? Is it a role that is beneficial for him? Many families, for example, have a scapegoat child, never acknowledged as such, but blamed for communal problems every day through the family's non-verbal signals. If you do suspect that your child has a negative role within the family, you have to take action. Look at ways in which, by altering your own attitude and body language, you can treat the child differently and encourage him to play other roles within the family. Bear in mind that you may be too close to the problem to do anything about it; if you want to get expert help, to rebalance the way your family interacts, professional counselling is an option (*see Contact Organizations, page 125*).

ROLES A CHILD CAN PLAY

There are many roles into which a child can step in particular contexts. This chart outlines seven typical ones, indicating what body language to watch out for in the child and in those surrounding him. Both are essential components of the role he plays, and if one set of body language changes, then the other will too. The chart also points out why the child adopts the role, the very real benefits, which must be remembered and compensated for if you attempt to change the roleplaying. Finally, the chart gives an indication of the likely outcome; many children change roles naturally with time as they grow up physically and emotionally.

	TOM BOY	CLOWN	BABY
What happens?	Girl keeps boy's body language (and interests) long after her age group has started behaving 'female'	Child is always the comic, tells jokes, makes people laugh	Child always gets looked after or indulged by others in the group
Example	Nikki, thirteen, is sports mad	Thomas, thirteen, plays the fool at home and school	Neil, ten, is tiny
Body language	Dresses like a boy; keeps her distance; movements are open and direct, with fewer wiggles or protection gestures than other girls her age	Tall and thin for his age, mobile face and body, 'comic' gestures and expressions that make people laugh	Typical 'baby' may be younger, smaller, weaker or show 'infantile signals'
Body language of others in the group	Dad and brothers give lots of approving smiles and eye contact. Mum gets irritated as she tries to 'feminize', with touch, eye contact, gentle voice tone	Friends almost always laugh at his jokes, act in friendly way to him. But also tend to laugh at him	Family and friends smile and touch more. They also hold him back from things, and sometimes ignore him in conversation
Why does this happen?	Nikki is modelling her body language on the most valued people in her life – the men	Thomas has learned to control others' aggression by laughing at himself	Neil likes being indulged; his family and friends like feeling in charge
Will the role naturally change?	May change naturally as biological maturity takes over, but why should it? Male body language is often more effective socially, so Nikki may benefit from her tomboy body language	May fade away with age and confidence in his own ability. Or may develop into a more confident version, where appropriate joking becomes a social skill.	May shift as Neil's body size or shape changes with age, or as his body language shifts with age or increased confidence
If not, what can change it?	Nikki could be encouraged to mix more with girls who are good at 'masculine' things such as sport, but are also comfortable with 'feminine' body language	Clowning may help to defuse problems in adult life. But he must develop an alternative mode of body language for when he wants to be taken seriously	He could stand taller, lower his voice, smile and touch people less and be more physically active

DADDY'S GIRL OR MUMMY'S BOY	BOASTER	MICROMUM OR MICRODAD	SCAPEGOAT
Child forms a special, physically affectionate bond with opposite-sex parent	Child claims to be best at everything, all the time	Child continuously looks after others physically or emotionally	Child gets the blame for whatever goes wrong
Charlotte, seven, much prefers Daddy to Mummy	Lesley, eight, always points out when she has done well	Michael thirteen, has two much younger sisters	Emma, seven, constantly has accidents, makes mistakes, attracts unwelcome attention
Gives Daddy hugs and kisses; acts younger than she is; flirts, tends to ignore Mummy or demand private time or treats with Daddy	Likes to be well-dressed, 'walks tall', often takes up more than her share of space at her desk, picks fights, is 'pushy'	Posture, movements and voice make him seem older than he is. He hardly ever uses playful body language	Clumsy, nervous and tentative. Her shoulders hunch, her face is permanently anxious, her voice soft and quiet
Daddy responds with hugs, closeness, eye contact. Mummy tends to be the disciplinarian, further making Daddy the preferred one	Some friends give attention; most others look embarrassed, with eyes sliding away and sideways smile	His sisters cuddle up to Michael and give him lots of attention. Both parents, in eye contact, voice tone and gesture, treat him as an adult, not a child	Others infringe Emma's space aggressively, borrow or soil her things without worrying, talk loudly and sharply, frown or look angry
Charlotte and Dad both want the closeness and attention this kind of body language gives	Lesley thinks boasting is a way to get status; others look up to her or feel emotionally superior	Michael thrives under the gratitude he receives. His parents like the 'extra adult' to help	Emma learned early in life that she gets things wrong. Others like having a scapegoat
May change as Charlotte grows up and finds her own friends, or as another baby takes over her special place with Daddy	Research shows most 'boasters' stop as they start to achieve more with age	Only if someone else takes over – maybe a sister	Will change as age gives confidence, or with increased motor ability
Daddy needs slowly to replace physical affection with verbal closeness. Mummy needs to spend special time with her, giving hugs and attention, and showing approval	Peer pressure can discourage boasters as they get older. Boasters may need support to learn the body language of genuine interest in others.	If the stress becomes too much, his body may call a halt by making him ill, or shifting body language to more regressed behaviour, allowing him to be a child again	If body language changes to upright posture, shoulders down, relaxed expression, clear voice – others will alter their approach

Pecking Order

In every group, be that of monkeys or of humans, some get to go first while others have to wait their turn. This 'pecking order' differs between groups. A high-status child in one group or situation may be low-status in another.

When your child is high in the pecking order, she will demonstrate a number of body-language signs that have parallels in the animal kingdom where status is dependent on physical superiority. She will stand taller with chin up and back stiffened. She will

A child may be the highest in the pecking order for a number of different reasons. A task leader has sharp, effective movement patterns, a social leader uses touch and eye contact, a rebel has exaggerated challenge behaviours. The enthuser (below), specializes in open gestures and body stance, lively expression, high energy and vocal variety.

move in a relaxed way, standing or sitting firmly and confidently, moving whenever she wants to, touching others without permission. She will often have what is called a 'plus' face: holding her head up, maintaining a straight gaze for long periods, and looking 'down her nose' – literally – at other children, even if they are no smaller than she is. Her voice will be clear and certain, loud enough to be heard but not defensively so. She will 'go first': taking priority in speaking, choosing territory and toys, interrupting more often.

In situations where your child is lower in the pecking order she will also use a number of animal signals but this time of submission. She seems smaller, tending to hunch slightly or slump in a chair. She will hesitate, just fractionally, before moving or speaking, checking with others, by a small sideways glance, before doing or saying things. She will often have a 'minus face', looking slightly away with head down, especially when a more dominant child stares at her. Her voice will be quiet or perhaps nervously

igh-pitched, or with a stutter or stumble. She will 'go econd', expecting to give way when speaking or hile playing.

Jostling for position in the pecking order often kes place, particularly when a child joins or leaves a roup. Between older children you often see xtended status contests. Most obviously, they will ght. More subtly – and more typically of girls – they ill try to outdo each other with outfits, possessions r number of friends. More usual are daily 'mini' tatus contests, perhaps in the dinner queue or in the layground. One toddler will encroach on another's pace or steal a toy. A battle follows. The winner takes n a 'plus' face; the loser retreats. One pre-adolescent ill challenge another by interrupting or touching. he challenged one stares the challenger down, pically jerking her head to shut the other up by xpressing disgust or disapproval, or making her take er hand away. If the challenged one has to speak ver the other child's voice or raise her own, she may e losing. The winner often speaks sharply to the ser or even 'punishes' the other physically with a udge or a push to make sure everyone knows she as won.

If your child is low in the pecking order in any one tuation, such as at play school, with friends or with amily, it is not the end of the world. The youngest or mallest in any group is often less dominant; age and rowth will sort it out as long as the child has some xperience of being in a group where she is higher in he order. Beware, though, if a child shows low-order ehaviour in every group she is in. Help her to learn ne body language of dominance so that she does not arry submissive signals with her into adult life. imply standing more erect or using more direct eye ontact will often make the change; this is probably hy, in Western societies at any rate, we instinctively ncourage children to stand up straight and look thers in the eye.

LEADER OR FOLLOWER?

Every group has its own pecking order, but only some groups, like street or school gangs, have a single, clear leader. This table outlines some of the signals that a gang of thirteen-year-old boys showed during school time.

LEADER	FOLLOWER
Wears fashionable, often expensive clothes that set trends	Wears, as 'tie signs', the same style of clothes as the leader, but not more expensive or fashionable
Extrovert, speaks out first in class	Waits to see if leader wants to speak before speaking out in class
When he does speak, everyone is silent; no heckling	Quieter than the leader; pays complete attention, with eye contact, when leader speaks
Can control followers by a look, a word, a touch	Shows approval of the leader with expression, smiles, and nods
Sets the pace in games, approach to classwork and how to react to teachers and pupils	Follows leader's behaviour, and his approach to classwork and games
Controls the pecking order of the followers by allowing more favoured ones near him and keeping lower-order followers at a distance	Jockeys for a place next to the leader in the classroom and during breaks
Gives favours such as attention, or special tasks	When given a favour, shows gratitude by expression and by 'posing' to others in the group

Working Together

/hat makes a group of children co-operate and oexist easily? One key non-verbal tool and signal of ositive co-operation in group work is matching, not nly when it comes to gestures but also through ppearance and mass movement. This is one reason hy many schools, youth organizations – and infor-nal gangs – insist on a common dress code or niform. It is also why dancing, singing or playing natching-movement games help make a children's

party feel good. A child's physiology is both stimu-lated and reassured by such bonding activities so he likes to be with others in the group.

What if one set of children needs to bond as a team in opposition to another set? Then territory is established, such as the cricket clubhouse or the street corner where a particular group of children gather. Codes of non-verbal behaviour – secret signs or special initiation rituals – make absolutely sure that no one from another group can join in. Finally, matching activities such as singing or dancing become much more aggressive and hostile, often with emphasized insults against the 'enemy' and accompanying gestures that pick up on fighting threats (*see page 80*).

Largely because of team bonding, the reward your child gets for being in a group can be very powerful: several times as many nods, claps, smiles, laughs and hugs than with a one-to-one friend. If the group is successful the reward is even greater. Studies have shown that touching – the most fundamentally rewarding activity for a child because it is the closest to bonding – happens much more with a winning team than with a losing team.

Coping with Groups

Groups have their problems too. What if your child needs to gain attention? Every time he wants to contribute he has to signal his wish to go next, not only to the speaker but also to the other listeners. His signals – a raised hand, open mouth or indrawn breath – need to be more obvious over a longer distance than in a one-to-one situation, and they effectively have to head off other people's attempts to turn-take. If the child cannot give the right level of

signal he may be ignored. Conversely, when he get the attention of the group the child may fee overawed by so much eye contact, closeness and non-verbal feedback. The result can be a nervou retreat; the child may stutter, his posture may drop and he may avert his gaze. All of these signs, so simila to those of the loser in a pecking-order battle, ma mean that the child appears ineffectual; and both h and the group will sense that fact.

If your child cannot quite make his way in a group feels uncomfortable or never quite succeeds, h almost certainly has difficulty in one of three areas. H needs to build confidence (*see page 97*), practis making contact (*see page 68*) and learn to survive th numerous pecking-order battles that a large grou involves (*see page 81*).

The key is practice. For a younger child it is bes simply to support him in as many large-grou

This class has managed body language so everyone can contribute by forming a tight circle to see each other's faces. Matching allows them to pick up non-verbal cues easily. And unconsciously they'll have chosen facilitator. to give a majority verdict gesture, nod or head point to whoever the group chooses to speak next.

CROWD PATTERNS

Crowds enhance all moods, and the stronger the mood, the stronger its non-verbal effect on your child. Different types of crowd create different moods, as well as presenting different kinds of risk. The chart shows some of the varied aspects of crowds, with their effects on an individual child.

	EXAMPLE OF CROWD	EFFECT ON CHILD
At what speed is the crowd moving?	Static – cricket crowd; fast – crowd at the start of the sales	The faster the movement of the crowd, the more likely the child's nervous system is to be excited and aroused, or irritated and distressed
What rhythm?	Slow – funeral cortège; fast – pop concert audience	A heavy, slow rhythm may soothe and relax; a fast one will excite or overexcite
What direction?	Random – crowded square; focused – leaving school	Randomly directed crowds are less claustrophobic and hence less distressing. If they move quickly, they may also offer more stimulation
Does it have a hierarchy?	One leader – school assembly; lots of leaders – protest march	A crowd with a leader will create more body matching, which is at once more reassuring and potentially more compelling; it is not as easy to break free of a 'matching' crowd. When a crowd has more than one leader, different subsets of body matching can all happen at the same time
How fluid is the crowd?	Blocked – crowd on train; fluid – marathon runners	A blocked crowd will reduce distance and increase touch which may both reassure and distress. Adults will know the dangers of blocked, moving crowds, and may pass panic on to children
What involvement does it have?	Spectator – cricket crowd; action – choir	The higher the body involvement, the more stimulation a child will feel. Add speed and rhythm for excitement – or over-stimulation
What relationship do the crowd members have?	Unstructured co-operation – airport crowd; structured co-operation – room full of ballroom dancers	The closer the relationship between crowd members, the more intense the situation will feel, and the more strongly a child's nervous system will respond
What mood is the crowd in?	Euphoric – supporters of winning team; angry – supporters of losing team	The strength of the emotion constitutes the real problem factor: a celebrating crowd can be almost as risky as an angry one

situations as you can find: play school, swimming lessons, children's parties. With an older child who may already have had some bad experiences to drain his confidence, begin with observation at a distance where it is not too frightening – standing on the sidelines at the swimming baths, for example. Get him to notice what is happening in groups he watches. Let observation lead to discussion of the skills and informal modelling of the key elements, such as making contact, getting attention, taking a chance to speak and handling jokes; encourage him to copy some of the body language he observes, perhaps 'rehearsing' it just with you. He may then be ready to try out his new skills in small groups where he is already accepted, and, finally, to start socializing in larger groups.

When competition is involved, every emotion can come to the surface. When the end result is uncertain, then not only anxiety but also some frustration and anger show through in the expressions and body movements of the supporters (right). When victory is secure (below), delight is mixed with near-violent movements that release the tension the children have felt, and show a high level of body matching and touching, typical of successful groups or teams.

Crowd Control

The body language of a very large group is unique, and the effect it has on your child can sometimes be overwhelming. Being in a crowd offers the highest stimulation level of all experiences: more people, usually in close proximity to each other, often intruding on a child's personal space with touch or eye contact. If you take two-year-old Annie to the shopping centre you expose her to high-density sights, sounds, tastes and smells. And unless a crowd is moving totally randomly there will also be a great deal of body-language matching on a large scale.

Stimulation to their sensory channels generally makes children excited, and all their attention signs are magnified. At first, Annie moves about happily, taking in everything. She also feels good about so much matching of posture, movement and voice tone between so many people, a magnified version of all the matching she has ever done. Finally the fact that in a crowd there is so much more going on can give a delightful freedom. Annie feels, often correctly, that she can run, jump and scream in a way she is not allowed to do at home because her behaviour will go unnoticed in the crowd.

For most children, however, the input turns into overload and the body matching makes them feel invaded and trapped. Stimulus-sensitive children will experience this immediately; it will take longer for others. Their sensory channels eventually begin to react negatively. Annie will try to cope with this herself by reducing the stimulation. She will turn away, snuggle up to her Mum or Dad, become withdrawn or fall asleep. If this fails she will fidget and cry, not only because these actions reduce her body's level of stress but also to demand that her parents do something about the problem or remove her from it. When the parents are trapped in a crowd – either physically because they cannot move or mentally because they choose to stay watching the parade – Annie may start to act aggressively, exhibiting hostility towards you. As she becomes increasingly desperate to avoid interaction, she will signal hostility in the same way as a loner does.

Added to all this is your own reaction to crowds. If you enjoy them, then Annie will too – up to the point where her personal stimulation barriers are breached. But even in the quietest crowd, if you feel unsure and are spotting crowd elements that make you wary of violence or vandalism, the child will pick up your tension and manifest it herself. If you feel like shaking with fear, so will she – and faced with a screaming child, you in turn may feel embarrassed or concerned. The result is a positive feedback loop of negative emotion.

What can you do to help? As always, keep as calm as you can, for as long as you can; keep your breathing regular, your body relaxed. Then, in the short-term if you have to be in a crowd with a child of any age, try reducing the stimulation as much as possible. Put hands over ears or eyes, snuggle your child safely in your coat or arms. High stimulation levels are a form of risk so protect her, as you would do instinctively if she were in physical danger, by keeping your body between her and the worst of the crowd. If you can get out and take a break, do so as often as possible; and once out, allow the child to let off energy and aggression by taking a run, or even having a mock fight with you. Afterwards make sure that her senses get compensatory peace and quiet; allow lots of downtime or 'trance' activities such as day-dreaming, more sleep than usual and a quiet few hours or days to follow.

COPING WITH CROWDS

Here are some helpful body language hints for an older child who finds himself affected by crowd fever, perhaps at a football match or disco.

Be wary when all these are true
- People are pressed so close together that you cannot move.
- You cannot hear your own voice above others'.
- You cannot 'hear yourself think'.
- The crowd is moving increasingly and you are joining in.
- Voices are getting deeper and louder.
- You feel uncomfortable.
- You find yourself saying or doing things you would not normally do.

What to do
- Shut your eyes; put your hands over your ears.
- Stop moving with the crowd by standing still.
- Start humming in your head a tune that has a different beat to the one the crowd is using.
- Make contact with an individual friend, give eye contact and a smile.
- Move far enough away that you can look back at the crowd or group.
- If you cannot do these things and are not with an adult, leave immediately.

CHAPTER SEVEN

CRIES FOR HELP

In one way, every body-language signal is a call for action: for attention, for solitude, for resources. Some signals, however, demand more urgent action than others. This chapter explores what we might call body-language 'cries for help'. It suggests what they may mean and offers ways in which you can best respond to meet the need.

Food Frustrations

Not eating, eating too much, not eating particular things or getting distressed at mealtimes: your child may well have presented you with all these food problems since he was born. But what underlies these symptoms?

They may well be physiological distress signals. Perhaps your child's body is not hungry, or is full yet being pressured to eat (a stomach is only the size of a fist, remember). Your child may be hungry but not for the particular food that you are offering. Studies show that babies instinctively know what and how much they need to eat in order to get the right nutritional balance, and a child who turns his nose up at one food and demands another may not be simply misbehaving but rather using this instinct to get for himself what he really needs to eat.

It may also be that some foods affect your child negatively but he is unaware of this or too young to tell you about it. Any of these physiological causes, not simple awkwardness, may be the problem.

You probably cannot go as far as some researchers do, offering your child every conceivable food and letting him pick and choose. With a younger child, though, it is worthwhile watching to see if he screams at the sight of one dish and reaches desperately for another. If so, you may be seeing a food allergy or a food need in action. Get an older child to keep a diary of negative or positive physical sensations he experiences after eating, then take your cue from that. Some of the most encouraging results with adults with food problems result from their relearning to eat just what their bodies want and to stop eating when their bodies tell them to.

An eating problem is often a signal of mental distress expressed in body language. You need to worry only if the symptoms frequently recur – the occasional tantrum or turned-up nose is to be expected from children of almost any age. If eating problems are permanent then consider these possibilities: the child wants attention or power and can only get that by being awkward around food; he has modelled your unhappy attitude to eating; the conflict in the family that often surfaces at mealtimes makes him hurt inside and he is expressing that in his behaviour.

With an older child who regularly shows eating problems, solutions are usually to be found outside the context of mealtimes and beyond the realms of what non-verbal support can offer. For if an energetic (and usually ravenous) twelve-year-old is distressed enough to use food as a weapon, he needs emotional

HUNGER RATING

Most over-eating problems start with a failure to tell when what is felt is real hunger, and when it is a need for something else (a hug, attention, fluid, exercise). Babies know this intuitively, but an older child may need to be retaught this instinct, to learn how hungry he is, how much he needs to eat and what food he really wants.

The stages of hunger are graded below. Decimal points have been used to show where the transition from one stage to the next is very small. A child should not need to eat until he is at, or below, stage 3 or 4, and should be at 3 for most meals. He should be allowed to stop at 5.1.

How hungry are you?
1. Wobbly, dizzy, almost faint with hunger
2. Very hungry, tummy hurts, grizzly
3. Fairly hungry, empty, know what you want to eat
4. A bit hungry, have a corner to fill
4.9 Just need one bite
5. Satisfied
5.1 Have taken one mouthful more than you need
6. Full
7. Tummy feels stretched
8. More than full, starting to hurt
9. Totally over full, will never eat again
10. 'Christmas Day' full

Family mealtimes are often the main theatre of war for family conflicts. Rory eyes brother Ben's identical meal, then begins to sink into a depressed state, shown by his slumped posture and need for head support. Ben's reaction, a slight smile, indicates he knows, and is possibly even enjoying his brother's unhappy mood.

WHEN NOT EATING IS DANGEROUS

Eating disorders are becoming more common, even in children. Boys as well as girls can suffer from anorexia (not eating enough) and bulimia nervosa (eating but then purging by vomiting or using laxatives). Sufferers are often otherwise 'good' children who react to stress with obedience and trying hard and a common trigger is often a further demand for the child to assume extra responsibility, such as the onset of puberty. If you spot any of these signs in your child, seek professional advice.

- Obvious distress and worry around food.
- Interest in food but reduction in food intake.
- Eating very small amounts.
- Cooking for the family, but not eating her/himself.
- Unwillingness to eat even small amounts, such as one chip.
- Hiding food, crumbling it, spreading it round plate.
- Calorie-counting when obviously already thin.
- A tendency to over-exercise.
- Frequent 'mirror-checking' – although obviously thin, has inner image of self as fat.
- Biddable; total lack of anger shown to others.
- Body-language signs of suppressed anger against self.
- Periods stop, or do not start when they should.
- Goes to the toilet after meals (to vomit).

support and help to solve his problem – or his family needs support to solve theirs. With a toddler, who often has great fun in tyrannizing mealtimes for months at a stretch, similarly try to solve any insecurity or need for comfort he may have in his life. If none exists, the issue is probably a power struggle between you and him. So get pragmatic. If he overeats or throws food, take it away. If he refuses to eat, shrug; as Dr Christopher Green says in the delightful book *Toddler Taming*, it takes sixty-eight days for a hunger-striker to die, and the child will crack some time before that.

When Sleep Causes Strain

Cries for help around sleeping patterns usually come in two kinds: an unwillingness to go to sleep and an unwillingness to wake up. What if your child is unwilling to go to sleep? The first thing to do is to check whether she is, in fact, tired. If the day has been unstimulating she may have very little 'data' to store and the body may refuse to let her sleep. Children's sleep problems often disappear as soon as they start play school and genuinely tire themselves out.

All too often, though, the problem is that the child is tired but will not give in to her body's signs of sleepiness. Nicki, aged three, 'taps her face lightly and shakes her head to keep her eyes open'. Reuben, two-and-a-half, gets 'slower and more deliberate as he tries to keep himself going'.

One 1989 study suggests that the reason a child

DEALING WITH NIGHTMARES

Nightmares are vivid bad dreams, often provoked by some recent event. They occur in the second half of the night and are usually signalled by very distinct body language. One questionnaire respondent described her child's 'tossing and turning . . . sweating . . . frowning . . . jerky arm movements . . .'. Nightmares can be remembered after the event, and the child is helped by your being there when she awakes from such a bad dream. Calm her down, hold her, talk to her. To prevent nightmares, make sure that your child does not have a hot bath before bed; try leaving a landing light on; talk through any recent distress or upset; and long-term, check her diet in case food is causing the problem.

Night terrors, in comparison, are near-hallucinations. Scientists believe that in the normal nightly series of switches from deep to lighter sleep (*see page 14*), the child's consciousness can become distressingly jumbled. She may wake screaming, will not remember what has happened, and be upset by your presence. In such cases do not hug her, which may startle her, but speak reassuringly. Specialists at London's Great Ormond Street Children's Hospital suggest you note down the time the problem happens until you have established a pattern, and then regularly, every night for a fortnight, wake the child up fifteen minutes before this time. This interruption before the night terror strikes teaches the brain new, less distressing sleep patterns.

Chloe ready for bed (above). Her slumped posture, slit-like eyes and comfort finger in mouth show her physical state and her rounded face signals to adults a need for rest. What a difference sleep makes (right). Her eyes are open, posture and movements energetic, her face-shape and skin tone signal alertness.

does not want to go to sleep is that some early experience has made sleep (or bed) a frightening experience. Perhaps a sudden noise in the dark or waking to find herself alone has scared the child. From that time on she feels nervous when bedtime looms, and the uncomfortable internal signals of fear drive her to do anything in order to stay awake. So make it safe and appealing to sleep. Stay with your child; or let her take a picture of you, tape of your voice or 'snuggly' to bed with her. Offer models of safe sleep by letting her see you go to bed; sometimes a very young child does not realize that going to bed (as opposed to being in bed when the child wakes up) is something Mummy and Daddy do too.

Reward a child of any age for spotting her own internal signs of sleepiness. Some typical ones are listed in the chart on page 90, but most children also have their own personal signals: Suzanne, aged four, rubs her thumb and forefinger together when she is tired, while Angela has a particular rocking movement that always precedes a nap. Sometimes these signals indicate a regression into younger years, a sign that the child wants to be taken care of as she approaches the vulnerable sleep state. Trish, thirteen, still puts her thumb in her mouth when tired, while many an independent teenager of either gender will reach for a cuddly toy to aid the falling asleep process, or snuggle up to you as they nod off.

Once you spot the first signs of a child's sleepiness, offer a relaxing routine that re-creates the body's natural internal signals of relaxation: comfort, slowness and a deep, low voice on the digital thinking channel. The classic ritual of bath, warm drink, snuggly blankets, story and lullaby reproduces this

exactly. Establish such a ritual about an hour before bedtime and keep to it, no matter what.

Finally, do not undermine your child's sleepiness by your wakefulness. If you say in a cheerfully brisk or tightly irritated voice 'Let's go to bed,' and accompany this by tense, nervous movements, this will not only stimulate her sensory channels, but may even start her digital thinking channel working overtime, with obvious results. Instead, try precisely matching your child's state, following her posture, movements and breathing patterns (*see page 34*); then gradually slow down your movements and lower your voice, and allow her physical state to follow yours.

The opposite problem to the child who will not go to bed is the child who will not get up. She simply may need more sleep because she is leading a hectic life that demands lots of processing time (remember that even at puberty, most children need nine hours of sleep). If this is not the problem, try encouraging wakeful body language. The body's natural wakeful-ness signals are the direct opposite of its sleep signals: a rise in energy; quick movement; a high, loud voice on the digital thinking channel. The classic signs of encouraging a child to wake reflect these signals. Try open curtains, bright light, a cool atmosphere and a talk station on the radio (avoid music stations as slow tunes can induce trance states). The child herself can help by stretching, opening her eyes, beginning to talk to herself – counting backwards from 100 if her mind cannot cope with anything else.

Finally, keep calm. It can be difficult if, at half past eight in the morning, your ten-year-old is not yet even up, let alone dressed. But, as with sleep-refusers, tense body language seems to have the opposite

DROPPING OFF, WAKING UP

Encouraging your child to listen to the body signals of sleep or wakefulness starts with teaching *her what they are. Below are some signs for you to look for.*

	A SLEEPY CHILD	A CHILD WAKING UP
Example	Trying to stay awake to watch television	Waking up on her birthday morning
Body posture	Floppy, no muscle tone, hands down by sides as body conserves energy	Relaxed but alert, body ready for action
Movement	Slow; head keeps dropping forward; yawns to provide more oxygen to help her stay awake; massages ears to comfort herself – she needs to feel safe before she can sleep	Stretches as body limbers up for the day; yawns to take in oxygen to wake up; makes active movements to get adrenalin going
Expression	Face shape changes with tiredness, becoming perhaps thinner or rounder as physiology shifts	Face returns to 'normal' shape, a signal to adults that sleep has been long enough
Eyes	Keep closing, cutting off visual input and encouraging her to sleep	Wide, blinking to open wider, a sign of body ready for input
Voice	Low and slow, or high and strained	High, loud and energetic
Inside	Thinking-channel pictures fade. Internal dialogue switches off. Body systems wind down. She feels heavy; her eyes feel itchy. Gets dropping sensations in body and hears snatches of music as nervous system randomly accesses thoughts	Body systems gear up. Thinking-channel pictures become clearer; child starts talking to herself again. Feels movement down centre line of body: a signal for action. Internally, may 'rehearse' what lies ahead, such as the sight of the party and presents, and the sound of music

effect. If the body feels invaded by your tension it may move into near-trance, cutting off the sound of your voice, blocking off the sight of your face and moving the child closer to a sleep state.

Signals of Illness

One of the body's main cries for help comes when your child suffers an injury or illness. The general external signs are often clear: tiredness, droopiness, change in temperature and colour.

There may also be internal precursors of illness, which only the child knows about, such as a certain feeling down the centre line of the body or in the extremities. Since he was two, one small friend of mine has always reported a tingly sensation on the outer edge of his right hand when he was going to be really ill. Now, at twelve, Stuart and his Mum are able to use this signal to pop Stuart into bed immediately, thus often reducing the symptoms and shortening

the length of the illness. Check, by asking if necessary, whether your child has such an internal early-warning system.

More specific signs of illness or injury are also clear, such as bleeding, swelling and vomiting. The chart on page 9 explains what the body is signalling when it uses these signs and what you should do about them. It also tells you when to stop trying to cope alone and get outside help.

The underlying message of many of the signals of illness or injury is exactly the same as that of a baby's distress call – to get your help. These signals primarily demand your attention: 'he will follow me around and sit silently . . . watching everything I do . . . very clingy'; or they involve regression signs – thumb-sucking, puffy infantile face, droopy limbs – to evoke your protective instinct as he did when he was little, and thus get the extra protection he needs.

Once help is there and the child knows it, minor symptoms often die down. So your first line of action should be to make your presence felt. Enter the child's world through as many sensory channels as possible, as you would if the injury was emotional (*see page 54*). Above all, use touch; every questionnaire respondent mentioned their sick child's need for this most basic of reassurances.

A final thought. A child's illness or injury may not actually be physical in origin but a cry for emotional help. When there are symptoms such as repeated headaches, tension, stomach aches, loss of bladder control, skin complaints or breathing problems, check whether something in your child's emotional life is triggering the illness. To confirm any suspicion, look out for other signs of emotional arousal (*see pages 46–7*). If they are present, try resolving the feelings and see if that helps.

Signs of Stress

When something over-stimulates a child, literally or emotionally, then the sympathetic nervous system moves into full alert (*see page 44*).

To gear up for an invigorating swim or a stimulating discussion, this preparation is appropriate. If the system is activated too often, however, or for too long, then the effect is negative. Organs are overstimulated; too high a level of chemicals is released into the blood stream; and, as white blood cells are less responsive when under stress, the child's immune system can become unable to cope. Inside, the alarm bells ring, making the child uncomfortable.

There are many possible causes of stress: overloading the sensory or thinking channels; a continuing

SIGNS TO WATCH

A basic guide to the body's main cries for help and what to do about them. Use it to remind yourself of *what your child's body signs are trying to tell you, so that you can act accordingly.*

WARNING SIGN	WHAT IS HAPPENING INSIDE – AND WHY	WHAT TO DO	GET HELP IF . . .
Bleeding	Red is nature's signal for danger; blood carries dirt and germs out of the wound	Raise wounded limb above the level of the heart and press firmly	Bleeding does not stop
Fever	Heat alerts you to a problem and helps kill harmful germs and infections	Get the child to lie down; keep him warm and still; dose with paracetemol; watch for fever fits	Child is confused, has breathing problems or stiff neck
Vomiting or diarrhoea	The body is trying to expel something, or take painful pressure off tummy or gut	Support child when vomiting; give small, regular drinks of clear liquid	Symptoms continue or include bleeding
Breathing problems	Alert you to 'hidden' problems such as infection, allergic reaction or emotional distress	Help child to relax in order to help breathing. Get medical help if you suspect infection or allergy; support emotionally if distressed	Lips are blue; child cannot talk; leans forward on elbows and cannot lift them without distress
Pain	Sign of damage, pressure or cell destruction; the body's way of forcing the child to keep on demanding help	Check for broken skin, and cover with dressing; watch for fever	Child has a temperature, is sleepy, faint or sweaty
Rash	This visual signal can be a warning to others to keep clear of an infection; or an alert sign of a hidden problem such as an allergy	Check for fever; if none then check for possible allergic reactions. Keep child away from school in case infectious	Rash is particularly severe or irritating or is accompanied by other symptoms

problem; a trauma or crisis; stress in surrounding adults that the child models; too much novelty; too little novelty. In all cases it is uncontrollability that is the key. So a room that is too hot is mildly uncomfortable for six-year-old Rosie but she can take off her jumper; whereas for Rosie's six-month-old sister heat will be highly stressful because her control over the situation is limited to a non-specific yell. For this reason physical causes are often more stressful to younger than older children. The reverse is true of mental causes. An older child can easily be stressed by thoughts of tomorrow's maths lesson or the memory of yesterday's playground fight.

If the problem is solved, then the sympathetic nervous system will ultimately be able to relax. If, however, the child is too young, too small or as yet too unskilled to act then the nervous system will remain on full alert. The body's way of coping may be to try to act, even though action is pointless. The child may start striking out at herself or others. She may show a series of 'intention' activities where she begins a movement then pulls back. She may fidget, fiddle with hair or clothes, develop a nervous habit or stammer. She may comfort herself with a repertoire of touching, rocking or stroking movements. One questionnaire respondent described a stressed three-month-old who gets 'tense in his upper back . . . tries to scratch his face . . . bites my hand'.

She may, alternatively, call for you. A young baby may use a special stress cry: a high-pitched, urgent yell. As with illness, a toddler may become helpless and regressed to arouse in your body the same nurturing response she used to. One respondent noted that: 'If he is really fed up . . . he will lie on his tummy full length on the floor and go limp, making it very difficult for me to pick him up.' Another toddler strategy is to stop sleeping or eating and develop the psychosomatic illnesses mentioned earlier in this chapter to get your attention.

How should you respond? A single instance of fidgeting or thumb-sucking probably means a one-off drama. If so, what she needs is a cuddle, some reassurance, the chance to tell you about it. When such symptoms continue, however, this treatment is just the start of what you can do to help.

With a child of any age begin by examining the physical environment. Make sure it is as comforting as possible with regular routines and predictable stimulation: not too hot, not too cold, with good food, early nights, some exercise and lots of reassuring touch. Then deal with the cause of the stress. If your child is young this cause will usually be physical and the above suggestions alone will remove it. With an older child the problem may well be emotional; if so, compassionate verbal support of the 'Why not talk about it?' kind may well be the key help a child needs.

It is also important to initiate daily relaxation to arm the body against the effects of an over-active sympathetic nervous system. One questionnare respondent revealed: 'We usually settle in a comfortable place for ten minutes every evening, perhaps in our pyjamas. Often we have some slow music on. Sophie lies on her tummy next to me, or sometimes half over my tummy. We play "tensing and relaxing" each part of us, and gradually get more and more floppy.'

Massage is an optional extra. You can gently but firmly stroke your child's hands, feet, face or back, keeping time with her breathing. Watch her responses. If a particular stroke makes her relax, repeat it. Avoid anything that seems to make her more tense or alert. And do not fight shy of the child returning the favour. Stroking your limbs or back gently will relax her almost as much as being stroked herself.

The main need of a stressed child is to control the input of stimulation. This boy shows typically withdrawn behaviour, with shut eyes, averted head pulled down into his hood, hands clutching the chains, arms protecting his face. His unfriendly posture effectively deters other people from interacting with him.

SURVIVING STRESS

This is a useful, instant technique for relaxing under tension, suitable for an older child to read and work through.

● What problem makes you feel bad: exams . . . taking a penalty . . . lots of people?
● How does your body signal stress to you: tummy wobbles . . . back tension . . . clenched teeth . . . ache behind the eyes?
● As soon as the problem happens or you feel the signal, take a long, deep breath. If you can, shut your eyes; if not, look down. Count from one to ten, tensing every muscle in your body more and more as you do so. At ten, you should be stiff as a board. Now count back down to one, relaxing everything and breathing out very slowly. At one, you should be floppy as a duvet. Keep breathing slowly, in and out. Tell yourself you can do this again as often as you need to.

Addiction Anxieties

Children who take dangerous substances usually do so because of the 'feel-good' factor. This may be a psychological effect: he thinks he looks sophisticated with a cigarette; she reckons she is being sociable when she drinks. Often, however, the feel-good factor is physiological: cigarettes give him a buzz; alcohol makes her nicely hazy.

Perhaps the main worry for many adults is how to spot such abuse. There are both general and specific body-language signs that suggest a child is taking substances. Most, though, can be concealed. A bright twelve-year-old who does not want you to know that he is sniffing glue can often hide the fact. In general, however, look for differences in behaviour: sleeping more, sleeping less, an up-and-down energy or

When children do something forbidden, their body language tries to conceal what is forbidden. Turning away, creating a barrier, putting head down – once these movements are used, they find their way into a child's general non-verbal vocabulary even in innocent situations. If spotted they will alert you to danger.

appetite level as well as any 'moral' differences such as lying or stealing.

How do you prevent or stop abuse? Most good campaigns nowadays aim to educate children about drugs and solve the problems that attract them to the feel-good factors in the first place. These are 'talking campaigns', not within the scope of this book (for relevant details *see Contact Organizations, page 125*).

Body language can, however, play a major role in deterring your child's involvement with substance abuse. Firstly, your general body language in relation to the drugs you use is vital. If, when reaching for a cigarette, your non-verbal communication is firstly anticipation, then relaxation and lastly contentment, your child will notice, even if you tell him that he should not be following suit. At best, seeing you smoke will create a curiosity about what cigarettes do and at worst it will create a desire to reproduce your all-too-obvious feel-good factor in himself. If you do take substances of any sort, point out to a child old enough to understand that there is a discrepancy between what you are doing and what you are advising him to do. Otherwise, as always, the non-verbal message will be much stronger than the verbal one.

Secondly, if you do discover that your twelve-year-old is knocking back a beer with his friends in front of the television be careful of your emotional reaction. Stopping what is happening is essential; but a strong emotional response while you are doing so may well increase the child's anxiety level around alcohol. The beer may disappear for a few years but when he does start drinking legally his body will associate fear or nervousness with alcohol. And guess what is very good indeed at reducing fear levels in the body? A more useful response is to ban the beer but keep the emotion level at 'annoyed' rather than 'totally panicked'; take things in your stride and put your energy into finding out just why your child found alcohol so attractive an option.

WHAT TO DO IN AN EMERGENCY

If you find your child collapsed, with (or without) evidence of drug abuse:

- Turn him on his side to aid breathing.
- Give fresh air if possible.
- Do not leave him alone.
- Get someone to dial for an ambulance.
- Take any evidence of drugs to the hospital.

DRUG SIGNS

This chart outlines the main recreational drugs (excluding narcotics crack and cocaine), used today and describes the body-language signs that may accompany their use. The first three drugs are the most commonly used by children before puberty while the rest are usually more relevant to an older age group. I have listed what the physiological feel-good factors are for each, as these are a large part of what you have to combat if you are to wage a successful war on your child's behalf.

KIND OF DRUG	HOW IT IS TAKEN	PHYSIOLOGICAL FEEL-GOOD FACTOR	SOME LONG-TERM DANGERS	WATCH OUT FOR . . .
Caffeine	Drunk in coffee, tea and cola	Increased concentration, energy boost, mood enhancement	High blood pressure, heart disease	Nervousness and irritation after not drinking for a while
Alcohol	Drunk in alcoholic drinks	Reduction in inhibitions, pleasant giddiness, mood enhancement	Organ damage	Intoxicated behaviour, recognizable alcohol smell
Tobacco	Smoked in cigarettes	Relaxation, stimulation	Cancer, heart damage	The smell; stained fingers and teeth; breathing problem
Solvents	Sniffed from glue or aerosol sprays	Confusion, pleasant giddiness	Accidents, suffocation, organ damage	Strange smell, intoxicated behaviour
Tranquillizers	Tablets such as valium	Calmness	Reliance on drug to stay calm	Child over-relaxed, constantly in 'downtime'
Anabolic steroids	Tablets or injections	Increase in muscle size and sporting stamina	Retarded growth, liver damage	Mood swings, increased aggression, loss of appetite
Cannabis	Smoked as resin mixed with tobacco	Relaxation, chattiness, reduction in anxiety	Psychological dependence	Same as with tobacco, plus distinctive smell, sudden bursts of hunger
Stimulants	Usually white powder, sniffed or injected	Alertness, confidence, overcoming tiredness	Worsening of depression	Broken sleep, no appetite, anxiety attacks, scratching
Ecstasy	Swallowed tablets or capsules	Calmness, energy	Worsening of heart conditions, high blood pressure or mental illness	Need for a lot of sleep after staying out overnight; thirst; dilated pupils
Hallucinogens	LSD paper dissolved on tongue; magic mushrooms eaten	Visions – good or bad	Possible worsening of mental illness	Sudden 'flashbacks' to the effect of the drug: confusion, panic
Heroin	Sniffed, injected, smoked	Warm and pleasant drowsiness	Addiction; need for money can lead to crime	Poor health, constipation, loss of periods

Losing Confidence

What we call confidence is really a set of subtle body signals that tells us that a child's body knows what to do. These signals evolved in monkey tribes because effort and support needs to go to those members who cannot cope alone, usually the younger monkeys. Those who do not need help have a way of signalling that they can cope, which liberates the group to turn its attention elsewhere. If, however, a monkey suddenly meets a situation it cannot deal with, it indicates this with non-verbal cues of a lack of confidence and the tribe rallies round until the monkey has gained the skill and experience it needs.

If your child feels fully ready for what she is going to do, she signals her readiness to those around her with signs of confidence.

Physiologists say that, not surprisingly, these signs overlap considerably with those of readiness for physical action, while the signs of a lack of confidence are very close to those of anxiety. Consuela, aged two, 'tucks her chin into her neck when she is not confident', while two-month-old Oliver has 'a vice-like grip' in such situations. The chart on this page gives more detail of the signs of confidence and a lack of confidence and also outlines the confused and

SURE OR UNSURE?			

Being aware of just how confident your child is shows you how to react and to provide help in circumstances where the child lacks (or has lost) confidence.

	A CONFIDENT CHILD	AN UNCONFIDENT CHILD	AN UNCONFIDENT CHILD TRYING TO LOOK CONFIDENT
Example	Stephanie, thirteen, climbing a familiar tree in the garden	Alex, ten, cooking tea on her own for the first time	Louisa, eleven, before a music exam, trying to look 'cool' in public
Posture	Holds herself straight, head up, ready for action; shoulders relaxed – no tension	Rigid, controlling the fear she feels; shoulders raised, spine tense	Normal, but tenses when no-one is looking; tapping feet reveal hidden tension
Movements	Goes straight to the tree, moves easily and quickly	Jerky and unco-ordinated; tries things out; hesitates	Over-relaxed; slouches deliberately to seem unworried
Expression	Slight smile, confirming relaxation	A slight frown, bites lip to prevent her calling for help	Deliberately blank, but nose twitches
Eyes	Looks straight at tree, taking in what she needs to know	Wide but defocused, or downward-looking – lost in own negative feelings	Eye contact normal, but defocuses occasionally when imagining problems
Voice	Calls out in clear, unemotional voice; laughs	Giggles slightly, does not speak	Speaks, but more quietly and less often than usual
Other body signals	Body ready for action; breathing steady; heartrate raised by movement not tension; good skin colour	Body ready for problems: breathing is quick and shallow, heart races, skin colour is pale	Body ready for problems but hiding it; breathes sharply at intervals when tension builds; skin colour is pale
The way the child reacts to others	Does not check to see if anyone is watching	Looks round to check Mum is there	Will not look at anyone in case contact reveals emotions

*The child on the slide is not yet confident, though the one
on the step is. Contrast the confident child's forward
lean and reach, smile, direct gaze and energetic
movements with the nervous one's slight backward
lean, 'balancing' arms, serious face, downward gaze,
static posture, and clinging to Dad's hand.*

often misleading body cues given by a child who is
nervous but pretending not to be.

What should you do about confidence signals? If
your child seems confident and is in no danger, leave
well alone. But if your child signals a lack of
confidence – whether or not she is trying to hide
those signals – then her body is asking you for
support. Like a baby monkey though, she is rarely
asking for you to remove her from the situation
completely. That need is conveyed in quite a different
way with more direct appeals for help, fear signals or
a simple return to your side. She is asking instead for
extra resources, skill or experience, so do not rush in,
denying her the chance to succeed eventually.
Equally, do not merely reassure; she knows she is not

CONFIDENCE BOOSTER

Recent sports psychology research shows that the
body language of confidence, used to boost
physiological preparation levels, can raise the
chances of success. Teach this strategy to a child
who feels she has a particular skill or knowledge
but who wants to feel more confident about using
that skill.

● Remember a time when you were really
confident about something. What did you see and
hear? What did you tell yourself? How did that
feel? As you remember . . .
● Straighten your spine, pull up; tense then relax
your limbs; grin, then relax; open your eyes wide,
stare straight ahead and slightly upwards; say to
yourself a phrase that gives you confidence, such
as 'I can do it.'
● Jog or bounce on the spot for a minute or two,
just until you feel the energy coming . . .
● Then go for it.

quite ready and your contradiction of that will simply make her feel in the wrong.

Begin by finding out what is needed: more skill, more practice, being left alone, being guided. Offer this at a distance if you can with words, eye contact and demonstrating movements. Going closer may undermine her by non-verbally communicating the sense that you feel there is a serious problem and therefore need to be near in order to rescue. Once your child has reached a level where she is nearly succeeding, and you feel that only the memory of past failure is sapping her confidence, then add the confidence-booster exercise (*see page 97*) to help her feel good enough to take the final step.

Family Crisis

A child is affected non-verbally in two ways by family problems. He may model the distress he senses around him – the tense stomach of anger, the tearfulness of grief. Boys seem more prone to such modelling than girls, and the more history there is of family distress the more sensitive a child will be in picking up adult problems from body cues. Secondly,

a child will start to feel insecure and frightened at any problem in the family, a natural reaction for any young creature whose environment is threatened. He will feel like this even if he has not been told openly that there is a problem; even toddlers can spot distressed body language despite calm and reassuring words. Children are particularly good at noticing when adults are 'masking' negative emotion, better in fact, than they are at noticing when adults hide positive emotion.

Three typical patterns of child response to a family crisis or breakdown are shown in the chart below. A child will often mix these, or use them almost simultaneously. It is often difficult to challenge them particularly if you are secretly unhappy. Yet it is best to be verbally honest, even if your explanation of what is happening has to be kept simple. Perhaps the problem is a marital one: 'Mummy and Daddy are cross with each other at the moment'; or some other issue 'Grandma is in hospital and Mummy is worried about her.' You do not have to explain to your child everything that is happening; often it does not interest him, particularly if he is very young. What concerns a child most about a family crisis is that, in his own

HOW CAN I MAKE THINGS ALL RIGHT?

Three strategies children may adopt to cope with family crisis – by keeping well away from it, or *subconsciously by intervening or reflecting, force the adults involved to resolve the issues.*

	IGNORING	REFLECTING	INTERVENING
What is it?	When child seems not to notice what is happening	When child copies and reflects the strong emotions around him	When child steps in to interrupt what is happening at any build-up of family tension
What does the child do?	Curls in on himself, hunches shoulders; keeps a greater distance from people so he does not see or hear them; avoids touch or eye contact in case this leads to emotional honesty; hides mouth with hands or stumbles over words; voice becomes lower in volume; claims he is fine; strong emotion not verbalized directly but shown 'safely' through drawings or reflective play	Reflects the anger: posture and muscles tense, fists clench; pushes people away; makes aggressive eye contact; voice always loud and high; feels overstimulated inside; resorts to self-mutilation. Reflects the fear: curls in for self-defence; clings; demands touch or shrinks away; voice low; feels stomach 'wobbles'; resorts to regressive behaviour such as bed-wetting	Deflects: gets angry or panics so that you turn to him; becomes as violent or as terrified as necessary to get your attention; becomes accident-prone. Redresses: moves in non-verbally to comfort; takes sides in a row; expresses anger or fear that family members feel unable to express

body, he is reproducing strong and painful emotions from the people he most loves. And if those people then deny that they are feeling bad the child is put in a double-bind: does he believe his own feelings or what the adored grown-ups say? As mentioned in the chapter on emotions, such confusing signals can lead to schizophrenia.

Explain very simply to your child the fact that you are feeling low, and that, if he has noticed you behaving strangely, this is why. Reassure him that, whatever happens, he is still loved. Then move on to giving him a chance to explore and express his current feelings, which may well be quite strong. Saying something such as, 'You probably feel bad at the moment. Do you want to show me how you feel?' can be a good way to allow a child to express the strong emotion in a safe place and in a way that will not frighten him or distress anyone else. Follow the guidelines on page 54 for how to cope and repeat the process regularly if the family crisis lasts for a while. And, as with any of the cries for help mentioned in this chapter, take the opportunity to go for counselling, alone or with your child, if either of you need it (see Contact Organizations, page 125).

WHEN YOU ARE UNHAPPY

These are the non-verbal signs of your problems that your child cannot ignore.

- You have an over-rigid posture, your spine tight and shoulders tense.
- You use overcontrolled gestures, particularly ones that keep limbs close to the body.
- You hold back words with tight lips, clenched jaw, an unconscious repeated movement of hand over mouth.
- You have slightly pink eyes and unshed tears.
- You increase your rate of 'comfort gestures', patting your own hand, face or body.
- You show an increase in downtime behaviour, and not even your child can get through to you.

This child reflects not only his own feelings, but also those of his parents; anger, in the matching of his father's clenched fist, fear and frustration in the protective hand raised to his bowed head, grief in his furrowed brow and sad mouth. The lean towards his mother suggests that he feels safest with her.

CHAPTER EIGHT

RIGHT AND WRONG

Naturally you are concerned about whether your child is healthy and happy. Above and beyond this, though, you probably want your child to have a sense of right and wrong. Is she learning to be part of society; is he developing a feeling for others?

A child usually learns about what is right and wrong in one of two ways. The first way is by experiencing reward and punishment physically and directly: being kissed for doing something good; being told off for doing something naughty; or being totally ignored (some psychologists claim that this may be more demotivating for children than direct punishment). The second way is by witnessing and modelling someone else's physical sensation: discomfort when hurt, happiness when helped. Studies have shown a clear link between a sense of right and wrong and the ability or inability to model other people's feelings.

Having experienced or modelled the results of behaviour, the child then uses this information. When she considers behaving in a particular way she either 'remembers' the actual reprimand or kiss or 'imagines' what it would be like to be another person feeling the pain or pleasure the action caused. The result, over time, is a set of physiologically remembered reactions to 'good' or 'bad' that can be triggered by even the thought of doing something – an internal memory of right and wrong.

Body language is an easy and effective way to help a child develop moral sense. Once she is at the stage of

Luke, accused by both father and brother, receives parallel sets of aggressive signals – pointing fingers, raised and jutting heads, an open-handed 'what do you expect' gesture. Luke's half-smile tries to defuse the situation with placating reasonableness, but his interlocked fingers show his tension.

being able to identify with others, get her to notice and imagine how they feel. The key here is to aim for a specific, rather than abstract, description of body language. In order to make the feeling vivid, pay particular attention to what is happening in the child's kinaesthetic channel. Your prompt might be something like: 'Jane is crying . . . where do you feel bad when you are crying? . . in your tummy and your throat? . . so where do you think Jane feels bad at the moment? . . can you tell from what she is doing?'

An older child will be able to apply the correct abstract terms to these concrete feelings. Questions to ask could be: 'Where do you feel guilt in your body? How do you know when you have done something good? What internal signs do you get if you have been accused of something but know you are innocent?' A child who is used to talking about what she senses inside may astound you by the number of different feelings she can identify, and by her inner physiological sense of right and wrong.

How can you use body language to find out whether your child has done right or wrong? The outer signals will reflect the inner experience. The feeling of 'right' is often a steady, firm, balanced and centralized sensation of comfort accompanied by an internal dialogue that gives a positive message. It leads to the child using a balanced posture, being able to meet your eyes and breathing steadily.

A feeling of 'wrong' gives the child sensations of imbalance and discomfort, probably affecting the back, tummy and breathing. You may spot this in micromovements of nervousness and discomfort: wriggles, fidgets, shifting from one foot to another, looking away or down, breathing unsteadily. These signals are very similar to those of incongruence because if a child knows she is wrong she will feel a conflicting mixture of emotions.

A final sign; if you notice a child giving 'eye flicks' – repeatedly shooting rapid glances in your direction just as an animal scans for danger – then there is a strong chance that she is doing wrong and knows it.

Telling Lies

How do you know when your child is lying? Many of the internal and external body-language signs of lying are the same as those the child feels and shows when he is misbehaving.

The body language of lying has some extra dimensions. The internal signs a child feels are usually somewhere between those he experiences when confused and the ones he has when afraid. This is the body's way of showing that there is a problem. The child experiences the truth through his sensory channels and it is decoded by his thinking channels. When he reports his experience in a different way by telling a lie, his body gets confused at its own behaviour and fearful of the consequences.

The child's body then tries to conceal the truth by hiding any body language that might reveal it. An eleven-year-old, faced with a chance to embroider the truth, may become very still so that his posture or gesture does not show the reality of the matter. He may take on a blank expression. He may exaggerate the opposite feeling from the one he is really experiencing (in one research experiment, students who were given both a pleasant and an unpleasant drink but thought they had to hide the fact actually behaved as if they enjoyed the nasty drink more). He may magnify the fidgeting or shifting movements children use when they know they are in the wrong; '(My child) always wriggles when fibbing,' one questionnaire respondent noted. And he will almost certainly give the game away if he talks for long

TRUE OR FALSE?

The more unconscious a body signal, the more difficult it is for a child to fake. To find out if your child is telling the truth, ignore controllable signals and look at the out-of-awareness ones. Desmond Morris, in his book *Manwatching*, offers us a hierarchy of trustable signals. The more trustable signals are less controllable; the less trustable ones are more controllable. The following list begins with the most trustable signals (1) through to the least trustable (5).

1. Autonomic – heartbeat; blood pressure; skin-colour change.
2. Leg and foot movements – tapping feet; minute aggressive or 'escape' kicks.
3. Trunk – look for slumping or tension in contradiction to words.
4. General hand gestures in the air – these show mood and are less controllable than specific hand emblems such as pointing or waving.
5. Spontaneous facial expressions – muscle tension, pupil dilation, movements at the corners of the mouth – are less controllable than set expressions such as a laugh or frown.

LIE-DETECTOR

Very young children believe the words, not the body, and so can be easily deceived. The skill of spotting a liar develops with age, but you can speed the process on by encouraging your child to look for the signs. 'Lie-detecting' others also encourages children not to indulge in lying themselves.

● Observe and discuss. If your child mentions that someone was fibbing in real life or on the media, ask 'How do you know? . . . There are clues; did you spot them?'
● Most children look at faces for lying indicators, but faces are very controllable. Teach your child to look at legs, feet, body and breathing.
● Encourage an older child to challenge a lie: girls are often better at spotting a liar, but worse at telling one that he has been spotted.

When faced with an annoyed adult, this boy automatically draws his body back into the sofa, raises his shoulders in protection, lets his face take on the blank stillness of concealment and keeps eye contact, not only to signal to the adult that he is not concealing anything, but also to watch out for any negative reaction from the adult.

enough because he will hesitate, give short, undeveloped answers, stumble and stutter as the messages from the brain to the mouth get even more confused.

Children are not born equipped for deceit; they have to learn the manoeuvres mentioned above. So your chief weapon in rearing a truthful child is early confrontation. Challenge him the moment you suspect he is lying and so undermine any chance of his ever mastering the skill. A good confrontation strategy is this. Move in close, then closer, keeping direct eye contact. Touch the child, perhaps holding his hands so that he cannot fiddle. Through this close interaction you will raise his awareness of what he feels inside, his confusion and fear. And by making him reduce all the little comfort and distraction signals, you will force the child to feel those feelings even more. It will be very difficult for him to resist the obvious way out of his problem – telling the truth.

Be sure at that point to signal immediately that you are pleased he has been honest, even if you ultimately have to punish the original misdemeanour. All too often when a child plucks up the courage to 'come clean' the immediate reaction is negative: a frown, loud voice, withdrawal. No wonder he does not own up next time. The bottom line is that the earlier a child learns both that his attempts at lying are doomed and that when he is honest he gets a smile and a hug, the lower the chances of his learning to lie.

Making the Peace

Fighting, whether between two children or between you and a child, divides into a number of distinct stages. Each protagonist will go through a number of possible escalation and de-escalation rituals before either the conflict disappears or a real battle begins. The chart on page 104 outlines the possibilities.

What can you do to control what is happening? Body language can help you spot the early signs of 'threat' and then judge, from signals such as skin colour, whether or not the fight is going to escalate. Bear in mind, however, that a red-faced child, though seeming angry, is in fact allowing her parasympathetic nervous system to calm her down. Sometimes, when

there is no danger, it may be best to stand back and let children sort out their quarrels amongst themselves.

If you do want to halt the proceedings try inserting a distracting or remotivating phase very early into the process. With younger children intervene to offer a toy, some food, a cuddle, or a 'grooming' gesture designed to get the participants more interested in nurturing each other than in fighting. Paying more non-verbal attention to the less dominant child is likely to arouse feelings of protection in the other. If you do this, you need to enrol and acknowledge the dominant child non-verbally so that he will not feel alienated; matching can be a good way. With older children a quiet word to divert their mental attention works best if accompanied by a touch and point, a non-verbal stress on the verbal distraction.

If distraction fails then try removing the protagonists from the scene of battle. Toddlers forcibly separated will scream at you instead of at their opponent but given five minutes in another room will have forgotten what the problem was. Adolescents, who often need to fight in order to 'de-bond' (*see Chapter five*), are less easy to separate, though one family I know insists on a successful, if rather odd, house rule that all inter-child fights be conducted by shouting through a closed door from one room to another. It works because cutting off a main source of input (visual) reduces the non-verbal impact, is not as stimulating, reduces feelings and makes it more difficult to 'pick up' anger from each other.

When battles are mainly verbal, particularly when the fight is between you and your child, the temptation is to calm things down instantly with a firm voice or some controlled display of authority. Studies show, however, that this may not be the most effective answer as it leaves the child 'in the air' with the sympathetic nervous system at full stretch. A better way may be to match the child or children and lead them into a calmer state.

The basics of matching are as before (*see page 32*). Copy what is happening, but remain in control; in fact do not try this if you are really angry. Mirror your child's posture, match his shouts in volume, speed and rhythm of words. Perhaps even emphasize these last two essential components of any verbal battle by matching them with gestures, tapping out the conflict with hand or foot. You will find that within seconds a 'conversation' will develop with each of you taking turns. Once this conversation is established, lower your voice very gradually each time you speak until it is at normal volume. This gentle way of leading your child out of distress will give the parasympathetic nervous system a chance to kick into action, leaving her, at the end of the tantrum, beginning to calm herself naturally, not physiologically high, dry and desperate. Then you can start to talk through the issues behind the emotions.

AVOIDING CONFLICT

Whether between children, or between you and your child, most fights never actually get to an active, physical stage in spite of the noise and fury, but resolve in one of these ways.*

	THREATENING	DISTRACTING	REMOTIVATING	SUBMITTING
Message	I can beat you	I've lost interest. Let's stop	Stop – I need to be looked after	I give in
Actions	Appears bigger by straightening posture, thrusting out chest. Adopts 'attack' expression of frown and tight lips, and 'fighting' voice and gestures, to frighten. The white face and deep breathing are signs of the sympathetic nervous system ready for action	Loses attention, seems to ignore the threat, fidgets, almost dozes. Voice is low-pitched and uninterested. The red face and irregular breathing reveal that the calming parasympathetic nervous system is beginning to operate	Threatening or staring signals disappear. Uses regressive movements: hand to mouth, wide eyes. Face becomes rounder, limbs slacker, voice more babyish generally looks and sounds younger	Lowers posture, looks beaten. Voice low, words dragged out and quiet, the opposite of a fighting aggressive voice. Hides eyes with hands, or in crook of elbow. Turns away
Desired effect	Opponent backs down	Opponent stops too	Opponent starts to nurture	Opponent goes away

If a fight does occur, younger children will quickly and easily become much more violent than adults – biting, kicking, and pulling hair are common. This happens because physical expression is still much more natural to small children than words, and because they have not yet learned the adult social inhibitions against physical contact.

Blocking the Bully

Bullying is fighting gone wrong. In normal, everyday interaction one child may get aggressive towards another but the other child will usually know how to respond. After a number of manoeuvres, such as those mentioned in the chart on page 104, the peaceful status quo will be re-established. A child who bullies will deliberately pick on a child so much lower in the pecking order that he will not threaten in return. In response to that child's attempts to de-escalate the conflict the bully will actually get more violent. In body-language terms a fight is like a dance with each child in turn threatening, distracting, remotivating, submitting. With bullying one child keeps threatening and the other keeps submitting.

The bully is often, in fact, a child unsure of his or her own power. A confident child will move easily in and out of status contests, sometimes winning, sometimes losing, but showing throughout a sense of balance and self-belief. The bully's body language reveals his self-doubt: dominance and attack signs are exaggerated; the voice is sharp, the expression hostile, the posture tensely aggressive.

The bullied child, conversely, is often one who, in the face of aggression, falls back instinctively on submission or remotivation strategies (*see page 104*). He (or she) will easily get upset, slump or cry but will find it very difficult to take on an expression of attack or genuinely to ignore aggression as in the distracting phase of the fighting process. With most opponents a child's alternating use of remotivation or submission tactics might succeed in stopping the conflict, but a bully just keeps going.

To make your child immune from bullying in the first place and to help him cope if it is happening, he needs to learn to stand up for himself instead of falling back on remotivation or submission patterns.

The message is only going to be effective if it is made non-verbally as well as with words.

Encourage a child to practise with you the body language of 'threatening'. This does not mean becoming violent but drawing himself up to his full height, shoulders back and head up, relaxing his expression and taking on a 'plus' face (*see page 80*) – with frowning eyebrows, smooth forehead and the lips in a tight, pursed line. He should drop his voice a tone or two to prevent it squeaking with nervousness and make it extra loud. When faced with bullying he might keep silent and make eye contact or loudly and

---

IS YOUR CHILD BEING BULLIED?

If you suspect that this might be the case, check for these signs.

In general
- Shyness; downcast eyes; unwillingness to interact.
- Nervous, fidgeting 'escape' movements; nervous ticks; easily startled.
- Temper tantrums or violence; starting to bully others.
- Depressed, slumped posture, often tearful.
- Sudden unexplained 'cries for help', such as loss of appetite or illness.
- Tendency to draw pictures that depict bullying.
- An increase in day-dreaming.
- Sudden misbehaviour such as playing truant, stealing or lying.
- Loss of memory or concentration.
- Regression: reverting to thumb-sucking, bed-wetting, needing lots of cuddles.

At home
- Loss of sleep; cries self to sleep; has nightmares; refuses to get up in morning.
- Asks to be taken to school; changes usual route to school.
- Very hungry at mealtimes (dinner money taken).
- Ripped clothes; cuts and bruises; strained muscles.

At school
- Stays near adults at end of lesson or during breaks.
- Meekly gives up allocated books or equipment.
- Watchful: stands in corners or against walls when out of class.
- Unwilling to speak up in class or contribute to classwork.

Often smaller children get bullied, but not always; if a larger child shows vulnerability, he will be fair game. Here, tears, downcast minus gaze and inability to stand square leave the victim open to attack from dominant classmates, whose confident and aggressive gestures intrude on his personal space.

ngrily tell the bullies to stop. He should not try to keep the fight going but get out, using his confident body language to protect him.

It is difficult to cope when being bullied. The non-verbal strategies suggested above will need a strong back-up of spoken support from you if the child is to be able to carry them off successfully.

There are also organizations that have been set up to help bullied children, and most schools will take action if alerted. But all the outside support help in the world will not work if, when faced with a bully, your child non-verbally signals submission.

Non-verbal Discipline

Your child has just misbehaved – directly, deliberately and with malice aforethought. What do you do? You may choose to shout, to smack, to take away a privilege or to impose a sanction. So where does body language come into it?

Although you may think you are disciplining your child with words, most of the communication you make about his behaviour is, in fact, non-verbal. These include disapproval, rejection, anger, sadness, mixed messages and capitulation, forming an underlying disciplinary medium that complements what you say, whatever punishment or incentives you impose. It can strengthen the words but can also contradict or undermine them.

To show disapproval the following body-language signs will underline what you are saying: a lowered face; a frown; a head-shake (possibly reiterated by a finger wag); a downturned mouth; a strong, sharp voice that says 'No'. All these contradict normal rapport signs and pick up on the status signs mentioned on page 80. They tell your child clearly and non-verbally that she has earned the displeasure

of someone higher than her in the pecking order.

You can start using the body-language signals of disapproval early: from the point at which a child develops control over her actions (around twelve months of age). This will mean that later in life just the hint of a frown or the suggestion of a head-shake will have the desired effect. One questionnaire respondent reports that her eighteen-month-old already reacts to just 'the voice' without needing any further sanctions. The only danger with a younger child is in continuing to use these signals after the bad behaviour has stopped and the disciplinary procedure is over. That gives a toddler with a poor memory for what happened even a little while ago, the clear message that her existence in general, rather than her bad behaviour in particular, is at fault.

The non-verbal signs that say to your child, 'I reject you' are a move away; a pull away; a look away; a flat, uninvolved voice. These signals communicate to her that you do not want to know her, that you are not interested in what she is doing. When your child is at her most infuriating you may feel that such ostracism is the only way to cope. If the alternative is violence then you are right. But the body language of rejection is a very distressing form to use, particularly with a child who is too young to talk things through. If you do need to cut off emotionally from the child for an extended period, make sure she has another adult with her while you are taking a break.

The body language of anger is sudden movement, an angry expression, a loud voice and shifts in physical functions, such as skin colour and breathing patterns. This is the 'short, sharp shock' approach. The message to your child is that you are at the end of your tether and she should stop what she is doing. As a genuine but infrequent sign of your frustration this body language works well because a child needs to know that adults get angry too. The communication underlying this body language is certainly more real and involving than the body language of rejection. Such anger should never spill over into violence; if you feel in danger of this, leave the room or ask someone to look after the child until you calm down. Make sure that your outbursts are infrequent or your

ALTERNATIVES TO PUNISHMENT?

Many children get most adult attention when they are naughty and are being punished. This can act as an encouragement to wickedness. Equally, children may model out an adult's punishment of them, thus learning to hurt others. The psychological school of behaviourism suggests that punishing misdeeds does not work, but that ignoring bad behaviour, while rewarding good behaviour, is the way to effective discipline. Here are some suggestions to put those theories into practice.

● Pull back from punishment. Clap hands and yell rather than slap; punch a cushion rather than a child; if in doubt leave the room, count to 100 before returning.
● Ignore bad behaviour. Shut down your body signals when the child is naughty: adopt a blank facial expression, flatten your voice, withdraw your attention.
● Reward positively. Use rapport signals – nods, eye contact, forward leans – as bait for calm, undistressed behaviour; big hugs and smiles for behaving well.

When children are punished, they model the punisher's state. What more proof can we ask for than this picture? Posture and expression are identical here, internal feelings are undoubtedly the same. When the boy becomes a man, he will control his child the same way and maintain the chain of bad feeling.

child will become used to them and they will cease to have any desirable effect.

You show that you are sad through a droopy posture; tearful eyes; low muscle tension; lack of energy; sad expression; a low and slow voice. Showing sadness to your child can be useful as, once again, it is necessary for her to see that her behaviour has a variety of effects on other people. Most young children will do anything rather than make a beloved adult sad but the danger here is the temptation to use this body language to restrain a child whenever trouble looms. If you do, you may end up with a child who can only be controlled by your being unhappy; that may mean long-term depression for you and possibly long-term guilt for your child.

When disciplining a child verbally, body language is sometimes used to try to cover up true negative feelings. Your body language might be a nod; a false smile; a tensely pleasant tone of voice. Adults usually do this because they want to soften the punishment. A 1978 study, however, showed that this particular combination of words and body language is the one that most confuses and angers children. Your child may much prefer (and respond better to) a quick, clean, congruent message of your disapproval, a fair 'punishment' then a swift return to normal happy relationships.

Mixed messages are also given out when you think you should punish some behaviour that you actually approve of. Your verbal criticism or discipline of the child is accompanied by a suppressed and genuine smile hovering round the lips; happy eyes that are trying to frown. But what happens? You will remember what you said and did on the surface and feel that you have done your bit; your child will remember the underlying non-verbal message and conclude that, in fact, her naughty behaviour was acceptable. It is better to make your body language and your words fit and discipline only where you sincerely feel it is needed.

Capitulation happens in situations where you want to control your child but are so embarrassed that in the end, you act only to keep her quiet. This classic 'supermarket checkout discipline' involves a cross voice, face and posture, then gradually becoming more and more exasperated but followed eventually by capitulation with a sub-

Here, Max's wholehearted hug, trusting closed eyes and smile at being forgiven tell his Dad that without a doubt he is truly sorry. In turn, Dad shows his forgiveness and acceptance of the apology by an embrace that is enfolding, strong and given with a genuine smile. Being close enough to touch like this allows both parent and child to 'breathe in' each other's scent and so further re-establish their bond.

nissive tone and posture. The final phase is often ccompanied by an actual bribe or the body language quivalent: a smile, nod or hug. This is a sure-fire way o train the child into misbehaving for life. The attern of body language will convince her, on a non-erbal level, that all she needs to do is keep on being naughty and eventually, before her very eyes, your esistance will turn to capitulation.

Discipline Directions

The key to effective disciplinary body language, in summary, is to be clear and consistent. When something happens that needs discipline, show your disapproval without rejection or aggression. For howing your non-verbal signs of irritation, sadness – or fear because naughtiness has put a child in danger - will indicate to a child that other people are affected by his actions. Move down to the child's level, literally, by sitting or kneeling, and tell him how you feel about what he has done. With an older child do not be afraid to show your emotions; he does need to know how you feel.

Once the bad feeling has been expressed directly, continue to be clear and consistent while you impose any relevant sanctions or punishments. Don't give in, placate, bargain, cajole or bribe, either in what you say or by giving jollying hugs or apologetic glances, which actually signal to the child that you want their forgiveness for disciplining them, and that you have very ambivalent feelings about their behaviour.

When sanctions or punishments are over with, a key element of disciplining your child is to show that you forgive, verbally and non-verbally. Once the disciplining is over, do not refuse to smile, hug or touch for days. If you refuse affection for days on end this will indicate to your child that nothing he can do will ever make amends for his sin. This in turn may make him feel that he is very bad indeed.

If you cannot offer genuinely accepting body language – you feel unwilling to cuddle the child or unable to keep eye contact with him, for example – do not try. This is your body's way of telling you that you are still angry or upset with the child. If you do try to cuddle or kiss, your incongruence will show and the child will know that you are lying to him emotionally. Wait instead until you can give true forgiveness, re-establishing your relationship with genuine hugs and smiles. Such behaviour is some-thing all children need to model so that they in turn can learn to forgive.

MAKING UP – FOR REAL?

A child wanting to be forgiven may or may not be truly repentant. Look out for these signs (which parallel animal appeasement signals) to tell whether or not the murmured 'sorry' is genuine.

For real
- Lowered body and head (animals use this to show lack of threat).
- Hand held out; hands held together as if in prayer; or an offer to shake hands (to show lack of fist).
- An attempt to stroke your hair or hand (animals groom).
- Drooped face and downcast eyes (animal sign of acknowledging a leader).
- Unconsciously behaving as if younger (to remind you of old bonding feelings).
- Hugs, cuddles, open body (animal sign of willingness to be vulnerable).
- Ability to touch (no threat, no resentment, feeling safe).
- Closed eyes while touching (feeling safe and no longer in conflict).

Not for real
- Mixed anger and appeasement signs, such as a smile plus clenched fists.
- Micromovements of aggression, such as bared teeth, or the fidgets.
- Deliberately behaving as if younger.
- Sideways glance or mocking smile, laughing at your credulity.
- Sideways turn, head turned away to hide mixed feelings.
- Pulling away from touch, in case it leads to real honesty.

Finally, what if you yourself err against your child? It is often difficult for adults to say 'sorry'. Or if they do say it, they do so offhandedly, on the run, with a resentful facial expression, or with an accompanying gesture of mockery, to avoid giving the child the idea that Mum or Dad is ever in the wrong. In fact, whatever your words, a quiet and genuine admission of your mistake – accompanied by genuine signals of repentance, will give the child the message that 'saying sorry' is a grown-up thing to do. Faced with a genuine apology, the vast majority of children forgive and forget instantly, and become more able to say sorry themselves, both in words and in actions.

CHAPTER NINE

GROWING TO LOVE

You start teaching your child how to love from the very beginning of life. At puberty, when your child begins to pair-bond, the foundations for success or failure have been laid for many years non-verbally.

Although much of the way you interact with your child is nurturing or protective, you also enjoy 'love play' in the broadest sense of the word, happily cuddling, kissing, nuzzling, hugging and tickling. More active than simply holding your child to provide comfort, this body language teaches your baby to interact lovingly: from soft nurturing through to rough-and-tumble play. Your child stores this body language in his memory banks until puberty when it is triggered off and used in the building of sexual relationships.

As your child becomes a toddler he continues to build his sensual and emotional possibilities through the world and other people. A toddler is constantly developing his emotional range and his interpersonal skills – particularly in this pre-verbal stage, in the area of non-verbal communication. It is at this point that he learns the value of eye contact, smiles, emotional expression and cuddles in feeling good about other people and helping them to feel good about him. He may also, at this point, go through a phase of creating strong bonds with friends of the opposite sex. He will cuddle, kiss, hug, tickle, fight, play and snooze with them. The sexual element is missing but all the body language signs of deep pair-bonding are there. All these social skills are stored away for ten or twelve years, ready to be reawakened when opposite gender pair-bonding becomes the most important thing in life.

Finding Out

Sexual curiosity begins at the age of two or three. Up to now a child has taken her own body and yours for granted. Now she is fascinated by the differences. She

Young children love skin-to-skin contact because of the pleasure of touching and because they feel safe when close to your natural smell and taste. Later in life when courting begins, they will often seek out a partner whose odour and skin sensation make them feel equally safe and relaxed.

112

may want to explore her own genitals and sometimes – to your horror – those of other children. She may happily watch a small male friend urinate, while he, at a slightly older age, will be equally enthralled by what she has not got and cannot do. Touching each other for sexual pleasure is not yet part of the game; what they are doing stems purely from curiosity. In private, however, toddlers often enjoy touching their genitals, pressing their legs together and rocking or rubbing against a smooth surface.

As your child reaches school age, development of the senses continues because she can now get sensual stimulation from the outside world. But actual touching drops off dramatically as she grows: typically from thirty-three per cent of the time during the first three months of life down to a mere sixteen per cent by only the ninth month, and then decreasing year by year until she starts to be sexual. Many children compensate by starting their own 'touching programmes'. Dominique, aged nine, 'always likes lots of cuddly toys to go to bed with', while boys may mock-fight in order to get the touch they need. Both sexes enjoy sensual contact with animals, which is one reason why keeping pets is most common from school age through to pre-adolescence.

The boy–girl friendships of your child's early years die away now, largely because it becomes more important for her to model the complex non-verbal patterns of her own gender rather than bother about the opposite one. She is therefore fascinated with her own body; many children enjoy looking at pictures of their gender naked and gazing at themselves nude in a mirror. Later, girls may undress and compare bodies, particularly when breasts start to develop. Boys may count pubic hairs as they appear or play urinating and erection-comparison games.

Sexual organs don't develop until puberty, but do exist in embryo in childhood and are capable of high levels of pleasurable stimulation. That babies are quick to explore the possibilities is shown by one study where ninety per cent of mothers of children under one year old said that their babies played with themselves.

Learning to Love

This whole process of development, from birth to puberty, is the body's way of teaching your child what he needs to know before he forms a sexual partnership. When and how all that knowledge comes together into sexual awareness depends firstly on when the child reaches puberty. It is then that sexual feelings are stimulated from inside the body through physiological changes. Equally important, however, is how your child has been taught to experience and think about sensuality and sexuality. When he touches a soft, warm surface or sees a beautiful flower is he able to give it the same

undivided and ecstatic attention that he did when he was small? When he uses his thinking channels to consider sex is he seeing wonderful pictures, hearing appealing sounds, experiencing a set of positive kinaesthetic internal sensations, telling himself that sex is good?

What can you do to make sure this happens? Firstly, give your child a wide range of good sensory experiences (particularly kinaesthetic as that is the primary channel for sexuality). You can also be positive about sexual curiosity rather than turning it into a crisis. Remember that such curiosity is there for a reason: to give the body knowledge for times to come. It usually dies away unless your outraged

response turns it into something to be repeated in the hope of winding you up. In fact there is nothing malicious about your two-year-old pulling his pants down in the middle of the shopping mall; and unless you have a real problem on your hands, at ten he would rather die than repeat the exercise!

Remember, too, as your child gets older, that there is nothing harmful about masturbating. He is preparing himself for a sexual relationship. As long as you have given him the right early experiences to help him put sex in the context of an emotionally fulfilling partnership, playing with himself is simply useful information-gathering and good practice.

When Embarrassment Strikes

Your child's sexual development is unlikely to be totally without complications. At some time in your child's upbringing you will embarrass him or vice versa. He will walk in on you enjoying a passionate kiss or you will get hot under the collar at an explicit reference on the television. The embarrassment will show very clearly: a change in skin colour, a sudden silence, an uncomfortable wriggle or loss of eye contact. The best – and least confusing – way to handle this is to be verbally open about it so that your child knows what is happening. Explain, if you want, that sex is very special and so it feels funny to be talking about it. If either of you feel like giggling, go ahead; that is your body's way of relieving the fear on which embarrassment is based.

What about explaining the facts of life? Unfortunately, because sex is so private for most of us we get horrendously distressed explaining it, even to the living result of that unique experience. This distress communicates itself through our body language, which contains elements of disapproval, fear and anger in our expression or voice tone. Rather than give a child the message that sex is wonderfully special we often imply non-verbally that there is something nasty about it or about him for wanting to know about it. The answer is to challenge those signs of distress by facing up to them. However tempted you are to deliver the whole lecture at top speed and

Truly mutual touching, as Aaron and Rachel hug. Notice the strongly entwined hands, equality in clasping, closed eyes and half-smiles – real joy. In a year from now these same children may well be avoiding eye contact and twitching with boredom or embarrassment if asked to play together.

WHEN IT DOES NOT FEEL RIGHT

Children need to develop an awareness of what body interaction feels right and what feels wrong. A younger child may not be able to make his own distinctions, but he can simply be given a set of 'never-with-a-stranger' rules. An older child can be helped by explaining:

● The idea of 'personal space': that he should allow only people he feels comfortable with to come very close – within the key 45-centimetre (18-inch) intimate zone.
● The idea of 'special places', such as breasts and genitals. Such places are his alone and no one else should touch them without permission.
● The idea of 'uncomfortable touching'. Being cuddled and stroked can, in some situations and with some people, feel nasty to the child and should be stopped, even if the adult wants to carry on.
● How to say 'no'. If in any doubt, the child should look the other person in the eye, say loudly 'Stop, I don't want that,' move right away and immediately tell a nearby adult.
● How some confidences should not be kept. No one should ask the child to keep hugging and kissing a secret.
● That in all cases, it is the people who try to touch who are wrong, not the child for allowing the touching.

with no eye contact, do the opposite. Sit close to the child, look at him, take a deep breath, relax and keep talking. Say how frightening it feels; your child will understand. If it helps, shift the whole scene outdoors where you can walk round a quiet park or along a solitary woodland lane and work off the physical discomfort, talking all the while.

On the other hand, an older child may try to deliberately embarrass you, trying out swear words or asking delicate questions to which he already knows the answer. The mixture of innocent eyes and barely containable laughter, or blank face and tense movements of hands and feet, will give the game away. Remember that the anger you may feel is a form of embarrassment, and probably the very result your child hopes for. A cool, bored reception with a disengaged voice tone, will eliminate the behaviour far quicker than a violent reaction, which only serves to encourage and prolong the bad behaviour.

Growing into Gender Roles

To form sexual relationships your child not only needs to learn about sensuality and sexuality but also about personal gender identity. A great deal of this learning comes from the words and concepts the child absorbs with age but an equally large amount comes from the body language.

From the moment of conception, your child's genetic inheritance determines such physiological elements of body language as height, freedom of movement and sensitivity to stimulation. These in turn create a predisposition to certain personality traits. Girls, for example, are often more at ease with people than boys are, possibly because their nervous systems are less easily overstimulated by interaction.

Your child's gender undoubtedly makes others see his or her body-language patterns differently. Other people will, for example, interpret a girl's actions and expressions as better-behaved than those of her brother yet they will allow the boy to show more of the body language of anger without telling him off.

The result is that, in general, girls grow up being more socially well-adjusted while boys develop to be more dominant and assertive.

Finally, the body-language models your child gets in life also create gender attitudes. From parents, from older children, from school books, from television come the relevant elements of posture, movement, facial expression. They all have their effect. Girls learn for reasons of 'politeness' to sit with legs crossed, which can make them look unbalanced and give the impression of incongruence. Boys learn to sit with legs apart, which gives them a naturally more symmetrical and dominant appearance.

You will want to teach your child the appropriate gender body language; but you will also want to avoid handicapping him or her with ineffectual non-verbal

Dorothy is happy interacting with Luke but on the left, Natalie doesn't want to play. Her eye contact and half smile show that she doesn't want to offend a good friend. But the pull-away and the raised shoulder give the message clearly and her arm across her body further emphasizes it.

Before puberty, gender signals are not really obvious; some pre-adolescents of both genders look remarkably similar in shape and size, facial features and hairstyles. Clothes often give the only real clues, and even they can be misleading as boys and girls adopt the universal teenage uniform of jeans and T-shirts.

communication. So, as always, go for observation, discussion and modelling. Beware though. Even nowadays a classic role model of ultra-feminine body language often includes large elements of submissive or placating behaviour while a role model of masculinity may well include patterns of loud, disruptive voice tone or strutting 'macho' postures. Adolescents in particular often begin by copying these stereotypes slavishly and learn only by trial and error eventually that they look silly.

Point out to your child that a likeable man often has some typically feminine behaviours in his body-language repertoire, such as a half-smile and head-tilt to indicate he is listening. And an effective woman may demonstrate some masculine body language, such as a direct gaze or well-balanced posture. The

GENDER DIFFERENCES

Body language of girls and boys becomes more marked after puberty. This chart lists some of the *main body-language differences between boys and girls of this age.*

	BOYS	GIRLS
Biology	More sensitive to light. After puberty, grow ten per cent taller than females, have longer bones. Male hormone testosterone strengthens muscles, but clogs blood vessels, and faster clotting leads to higher blood pressure	More sensitive to sound, better sense of smell. Have twice the body fat of males after puberty. Female hormones create more 'positive' cholesterol so blood vessels are more elastic. Less affected by infections
Use of space	Need more space than girls, even before they grow physically bigger. Invade personal space more. More vulnerable to being approached from the front	Learn postures that take up less space; move out of the way more often. Allow others to approach them more closely. More vulnerable to being approached from the side
Movement	More active; evidence suggests this starts in the womb. Learn open, away-from-body movements	Early in life, have more pronounced body movements but with socialization, learn closed, reserved body movements
Expression	Smile less; researchers disagree as to whether this is a sign of leadership or lack of self-confidence	Smile more; hide uncomfortable feelings more than boys do
Eye contact	Slightly bigger eyes; blink faster and more regularly, and look away more. Less active tear glands make them less likely to cry	Eyebrows higher, more often raised, giving a more appealing, socially responsive look. Eyes show greater proportion of white, so seem to show more emotion. Look at people more
Speech	Talk more often than girls and for longer. Interrupt, change the subject and 'talk over' more than girls do. Use more commands and definite statements	Talk less, interrupt less, give 'it is your turn' signals more often. Hesitate and stammer more. Use more questions and tentative statements
Touch patterns	Touch girls more often than vice versa, but with status-proving rather than friendly movements	More willing to touch to comfort; use touch less often to control
Internal feelings	From birth, feel internal signs of emotion more; show external signs of emotion less	From birth, feel internal signs of emotion less, show external signs of emotion more
Responses to others	From birth, less likely to respond to others with eye contact, smiles or nods. Boys seem to interpret adults' behaviour as more disapproving – possibly because, in response to boys' seeming lack of social interest, adults may act more negatively towards them	From birth, more able to read people and their emotions from body language; in evolutionary terms, perhaps this helped mothers survive and protect their young

best idea is to 'borrow' from both genders the elements that work and combine them to make a successful whole.

Finally, check out your own personal preconceptions about gender body language. Are you expecting children to do what you do? Particularly if you are more than twenty-five years older than your child, your natural repertoire of facial expressions, pos-

tures and gestures may be dated or even ineffectual. Girls today, for example, tend to speak at a lower tone than their mothers did, a non-verbal development which generally makes them sound more confident and in control at an earlier age. So don't push your children to copy your gender body language – get them, instead, to emulate role models closer to their own age group.

The Challenge of Puberty

The real shift from androgenous childhood to gender-specific adolescence happens at puberty. For both boys and girls massive body changes occur to prepare them for child-rearing. Suddenly your son's arm may be half an inch longer so when he reaches out for a cup he knocks it over. Overnight your daughter has to cope with developed hips and top-heaviness so she starts to waddle when she runs. Every aspect of body language becomes awkward until young people get used to their different size, shape and weight.

The young person also starts to become more aware of personal body image and to compare it with a media ideal. This immediately results in a desperate attempt either to hide or to flaunt. Boys who have grown four inches taller in the last year curve their shoulders and bow their heads or walk taller and strut. Girls with budding breasts start to lean in or thrust their chests out and wiggle.

Your child's body language may also change with the direct reminders of new maturity. Sudden erections can lead to a sudden spate of embarrassed exits.

A typical pre-adolescent combination of both attraction and wariness. Their distance, crossed arms and lack of facial expression could mean mistrust. But their posture, head direction and gaze are turned towards each other, their crossed arms match gesture, and the girl certainly shows a half smile.

Periods can make your previously placid fourteen-year-old suddenly temperamental. All the more specifically sexual signs make your adolescent less confident about identity and independence; body language may reflect this with the appearance of sudden nervous habits, the disappearance of rapport signals and a severing of bonding signs.

You can help non-verbally by not appearing alienated when your child draws back and literally demands more body space. You can reassure with continuing signals of affection, even when the child's own rapport skills are in abeyance for a while. You can stay unembarrassed by your child's embarrassment over the signs of puberty, and discuss ways of using body language to cope with the resulting new shape. Do not panic. In a few years, a confident adult will reappear.

119

A GUIDE TO FLIRTING

This chart demonstrates how Annette, fourteen, uses the 'come-on' and 'pull-back' when talking to her brother's fifteen-year-old friend. Observe your own teenager for similar behaviour.

	THE COME-ON	THE PULL-BACK
Closeness	Comes within arm's length of him, leaning across to reach the toaster	He moves forwards, so she backs off, then returns to stand close
Angle	Faces him directly	Keeps turning away, fiddling with cutlery
Eyes	Keeps eye contact most of the time	Lets gaze slide away from him, then looks back with a smile.
Expression	Smiles, laughs more than usual	Mock-frowns at his remarks
Voice	Pitch drops	Lets her voice rise when she is pretending to be angry
Touch	Reaches out and pats his arm to emphasize words	Pulls away with a flounce when he puts his hand out to her

Display behaviours for young people today are subtly different from those of previous generations. In this age of equality, girls may adopt almost masculine display positions, legs wide and shoulders square, arms protecting of their bodies rather than held back to better display breasts and waists. Boys' display posture has softened and now includes more 'attention' elements, with head turned towards the woman when she speaks. Remnants of feminine tradition remain obvious in this group of teenagers. The girl in the striped sweatshirt uses a classic female 'hair-grooming' display gesture and two of the girls use the exaggerated 'upward looking' listening glance that women often use to signal interest.

Displaying Interest

Even before puberty your child may show an interest in the opposite sex. This starts, often as early as nine or ten for girls, when young people gather to talk. But the object of the exercise is not to play, as it was a few months earlier. The object is to look at 'the others' and to be looked at in return.

The vast majority of the complex and incredibly exciting ritual of showing off, 'chatting up' and getting together is done non-verbally. The body language used here is partly instinctive and reflects the courtship rituals that many primates use; much of it, however, is learned and differs from culture to culture and generation to generation. Research proves, for example, that there has been a huge shift in Western society since the sexual revolution; touching happens a lot sooner than it used to in a boy–girl friendship.

The pattern usually begins with a 'display'. Same-sex groups gather to talk. Groups may be static but will usually find some reason to move around a lot – maybe a mock-fight or a game – so getting to look at each other. They will offer 'displays', slightly exaggerated movements designed to show off their best points at a distance. Questionnaire respondents who saw their children in mixed-sex groups reported that 'she . . . tosses her hair back . . . laughs . . . he stands tall . . . looks "mean" . . .'.

During all this, your child will be nervously deducing who interests him and who seems interested in him. He will look across at different possible partners (the whites of eyes are specially designed to show at a distance who is the object of desire) then he will half-turn towards the chosen one. As soon as he notices that the gaze is returned he will start to pose:

All four young people are friends – taking up the same body posture even to the interlocking fingers. But their grouping, smiles, body leans, touches and eye contact show clearly who is paired with whom, though the couple to the right show wider smiles more typical in a newer relationship.

These two have had a relationship, but it is now in trouble. Their physical ease with each other, suggesting an existing relationship, is shown by the way they are happy touching shoulders with no sense of surprise or intrusion. But the slumped posture, blocking arms across waists and lowered heads show a negative mood. They are literally turning away from each other. His stare into the middle distance, her stare down at the floor suggest they are 'internal' in their thoughts, processing what has happened, while their facial expressions suggest a mixture of anger and sadness. Whether they make up or break up is impossible to judge, but their body language makes clear that they are having problems.

an extra laugh, a really 'cool' expression. Then after a few minutes comes a glance across to check that the potential partner is still interested. If so, a longer-than-usual stare followed by a look away, signals real interest. The next step is to move closer and find an excuse to talk.

Rejection Signs

When someone is uninterested what are the signals? The body-language in this area is often confusing. Showing eagerness non-verbally is considered a sign of social incompetence by many adolescents so they often try to appear uninterested. They may, however, simply be shy. All too often, then, your child may think she has made no impression when, in fact, the potential partner is keen. Alternatively, she will think she has been encouraged when she has actually been rejected. When the desperate cry is, 'I don't know if he's interested, Mum,' then she needs to observe the body language, not the words.

If the apparent signs of non-interest – looking away, silence, curt voice tone – are accompanied by signs of nervousness (skin-colour change, fidgeting, downcast eyes) then he is eager. If the seeming signs of interest are accompanied by signs of hostility (slight mouth movements of anger, raised shoulders, sharp voice tone) or of boredom (stifled yawns, distracted gaze) then all is lost.

Young people's attempts to attract can actually deter. Boys all too often think that the way to impress is to strut, with high gaze and head up. They will talk too much, too loudly and too quickly because, with other boys, these are status signals. But to girls, this all means that a boy is not going to provide comfortable body language with equal turn-taking in conversation, smiles and eye contact. Girls may giggle from nervousness, and a less-than-confident boy will then be convinced that they will giggle at him.

You can help in all these areas by getting your child to talk about what works. You cannot model effective 'display' behaviour because adult body language is different from that of early adolescence. What will help, however, is discussing with your child what she has tried and how much it has achieved. Being able to talk to you about what her object of desire did and how he did it will support your child to interpret the body-language signals correctly. For you, the immense sense of excitement, possibility and sheer emotional intensity that your child will feel at this vital time in her life is something not to be missed.

SAYING 'NO'

It is often difficult, particularly when intimate relationships are a new skill, for young people to refuse something, be it an offer of a date, an emotional commitment or a sexual suggestion. Girls, in particular, often mix messages, so that what is meant as 'no' comes over as 'yes' and leads to later trouble. Here are some body-language rules for clean, effective refusal, based on English writer Anne Dickson's assertiveness work.

Do
- Face the other person directly.
- Stand back slightly.
- Hold eye contact, but give no smile.
- Keep voice level and balanced.
- Shake head slightly to give an unconscious 'no' message as well as a verbal one.

Do not
- Face away and avoid eye contact so other person cannot tell if you mean it.
- Smile, so you give a mixed message.
- Say your words of refusal quickly and with a nervous laugh as if you mean 'no now, yes later'.
- Use a low, soft voice, leaning forward and touching, thus undermining the 'no' message completely.

First Touch

When distance turns to closeness pre-adolescents nowadays can adopt a very slow pace. Having displayed, made eye contact, found an excuse to talk, and discovered a mutual liking, there will probably be quite an extended period of getting to know each other, 'hanging out with the crowd', going to places where they can do things together. The aim of this time is not only to get to know each other through words but also non-verbally.

They will look at each other much more than at anyone else, gazing even when they think the other one is not looking. They will be happier to move closer, matching more and more. It will all feel wonderful, and incredibly insecure. Then they will find an excuse to bridge the gap to a first touch.

At the end of childhood, after a long period when touching has been decreasing and touching of the opposite sex has been almost non-existent for years, this is a big step. In order to avoid any danger of rejection, most young people slide gradually into the first touch through a series of what one questionnaire respondent called 'pretend touches', excuses to make contact which, if spurned, can be excused as a mistake or a misunderstanding. They will nudge, lean across to reach something, push and mock-fight. They may behave like younger children to give them an excuse for hugs or full body snuggles.

Even before the first touch is made your child may have been aware of 'adult' feelings. Once that touch is made, however, and the realization dawns of just what it is like to make contact, then nothing is the same again. The child's body will be responding to a new and unbelievably exciting set of stimuli; and if this happens with someone liked and trusted then the result will be sexual pleasure in body and in mind.

Once that bridge has been crossed young people typically move into a period of intense bonding which is very similar to that between you and your baby when it first comes into the world. It involves huge amounts of 'motion tracking': moving together as they run, jump, chase and dance; lots of touch: holding hands in public, walking arm in arm, sudden hugs, even when walking along. In private it involves more and more face-to-face contact and eye contact for long periods of time; stroking and patting hands, arms and faces; and a special low, soft voice tone that they use only with each other, reminiscent of the special tone that you probably used in the first few years of your child's life.

At some point in all this will come the first kiss. It is usually tentative, particularly if this is a first time for both young people. It is often gentle, unsure, incredibly tender and always very, very special.

Suddenly you have to realize that your child is growing up. Your teenager will now move at the best pace into whatever sensual, emotional and sexual relationship is right. And if, over the past thirteen or fourteen years, you have laid the foundations for a happy and fulfilled love life then, at this point, your job is easy. Simply stand back, and celebrate.

All the signs of close pair bonding show clearly here. She has a broad, genuine, teeth-showing smile, with head tilted up to receive the kiss. He leans in to make more body contact and provide support. Both have eyes closed in trust and the better to enjoy the wonderfully new and exciting sensations that surround a growing relationship.

RESOURCES

CONTACT ORGANIZATIONS

UK

Asian Family Counselling Service, 74 The Avenue, London W13 8LB (081 997 5749).

British Association of Counselling, 1 Regent Place, Rugby, Warwickshire CV21 2PJ (0788 578328/9).

Carelines 081 514 1177 (London); 0532 45656 (Leeds); 021 456 4560 (Birmingham).

Institute of Family Therapy, 43 New Cavendish Street, London W1M 7RG (071 935 1651).

The Parent Network, 44–46 Caversham Road, London NW5 2DS (071 485 8535). National organization offering training in parenting skills.

Parentline 0268 757077. Listening service for parents with worries of any kind.

Parents Anonymous 071 263 8918. Listening service for parents, which also has referral numbers for specific difficulties.

Relate (National Marriage Guidance Council), Herbert Gray College, Little Church Street, Rugby, Warwickshire CV21 3AP (0788 573241).

Youth Access, Magazine Business Centre, 11 Newark Street, Leicester LE1 5SS (0533 558763).

Childline, Freepost 1111, London N1 0BR (0800 1111). Free helpline for children in difficulties.

Children Protection Helpline 0800 800500. Free helpline, to protect children from physical, emotional or sexual abuse.

Crysis, London WC1N 3XX (071 404 5011). Offers counselling and advice if your baby cries too much.

Eating Disorders Association 0603 621414. Offers help with anorexia and bulimia nervosa.

Gingerbread, 35 Wellington Street, London WC2 7BN (071 240 0953). Can put you in touch with a network of local self-help groups for single parents.

Incest Crisis Line, PO Box 32, Northolt, Middlesex UB5 4JC (081 890 4732). Helpline for adults and children suffering from abuse.

Institute of Drama Therapy, PO Box 32, Stratford-upon-Avon CV37 6GU (071 831 4763). Can put you in touch with therapists who use drama with the emphasis on non-verbal techniques.

Kidscape, 152 Buckingham Palace Road, London SW1W 9TR (071 730 3300). Help for children suffering violence and abuse.

National Association for Gifted Children, Park Campus, Boughton Green Road, Northampton NN2 7AL (0604 792300). Help for gifted children and their parents.

Release, 388 Old Street, London EC1V 9LT (071 603 8654). Help on drug issues.

Society of Teachers of Alexander Technique, 20 London House, 266 Fulham Road, London SW10 9EL (071 351 0828). Will refer you to an Alexander Technique teacher in your area.

USA

American Association of Marriage and Family Therapy, 1100 17th Street NW, 10th Floor, Washington DC 20036 (202 452 0109).

Institute of Marriage and Family Relations, 6116 Rolling Road, Suite 316, Springfield, VA 22152 (703 569 2400).

National Council on Family Relations, 3989 Central Avenue, NE Suite 550, Minneapolis MN 55421 (612 781 9331).

American Association for Counseling and Development, 5999 Stevenson Avenue, Alexandria UA (202 304 3398).

Child Welfare League of America, 440 First Street, NW Suite 310, Washington DC 20009.

Family Service America Inc, 11700 West Lake Park Drive, Milwaukee WI (224 3099).

AUSTRALIA

Anorexia and Bulimia Nervosa Foundation, 1513 High Street, Glen Innes NSW 2370 (067 885 0318).

Child Abuse Prevention Service, 13 Norton Street, Ashfield NSW 2131 (02 716 8000).

Child Protection Council, 4th Floor, Remington Centre, 169–183 Liverpool Street, Sydney NSW 2000 (008 04 4848).

Family Support Services Association, 2 Wunda Street, Concord West NSW 2138 (02 743 6565).

Lifeline Counselling, 53 Regent Street, Sydney NSW 2000 (02 951 5555).

Youth Insearch Australia Inc, 43 Garfield Road, Riverstone NSW 2765 (02 627 4104).

Youthline Sydney, 53 Regent Street, Sydney NSW 2001 (02 951 5522).

Child and Family Care Network, 583 Ferntree Gully Road, Glen Waverley VIC 3150 (03 560 0188).

Child and Family Centre, 480 St Kilda Road, St Kilda VIC 3182 (03 529 8799).

Child Protection Branch, 24 Hour Crisisline (03 13 1278).

Child Welfare and Family Support Service Berry Street Inc, 1 Berry Street, East Melbourne VIC 3002 (03 429 9266).

Family Therapy Centre, 368 Haughton Road, Clayton VIC 3168 (03 562 8766). For the Oakleigh area.

Youth at Risk, 67 Inkerman Street, St Kilda VIC 3182 (03 525 5902).

Anorexia and Bulimia Nervosa Support Group, Friendship House, 20 Balfour Street, New Farm QLD 4005 (07 358 4224).

Sexual Abuse Information and Support Link, 22 Hurworth Street, Bowen Hills QLD 4006 (07 852 2506).

Youth Welfare and Guidance Clinics (07 397 9077, 07 208 7599).

Anorexia Bulimia Nervosa Association, 35 Fullerton Road, Kent Town SA 5067 (08 362 6772).

Child Adolescent and Family Health Service, 295 South Terrace, Adelaide SA 5000 (08 236 0400, 08 236 0444) 24 hour service.

Children's Resource Centre, 149 Kermode Street, North Adelaide SA 5006 (08 267 3830).

Children's Services, 31 Flinders Street, Adelaide SA 5000 (08 226 0044).

Anorexia and Bulimia Support Group, PO Box 773, Woden ACT 2606 (062 86 3941, 062 81 8315).

Department of Community Services, Child Protection and Family Crisis Service, Southern Highlands Area Office (062 99 4546, 008 42 5288).

Youth Information Service, Civil Youth Centre, Cooyong Street, Canberra ACT 2600 (062 57 1515).

Youthline, 69 Northbourne Avenue, Canberra ACT 2600 (062 57 2333).

Australian Association of Marriage and Family Counsellors, 41 Cabarita Road, Armadale, WA 6112.

Department for Community Development, 189 Royal Street, East Perth WA 6004 (09 222 2555). For Family Crisis Programmes, Youth Activity Programmes and Child Protection Services.

Youth Insearch Inc, 15 Lawrence Avenue, West Perth WA 6005 (09 321 1711).

Youthline Samaritans, 60 Bagot Road, Subiaco WA 6008 (09 388 2500).

Department of Health and Community Services, Wyadra, 20 Clare Street, New Town TAS 7008 (002 78 4149).

FURTHER READING

Neill, Sean. *Classroom Non-verbal Communication*, London, Routledge 1991

Welch, Dr Martha. *Holding Time*, London, Century

O'Connor, J. & Seymour, J. *Introducing Neuro-linguistic Programming*, London, Aquarian, 1993

Lewis, B.A. & Pucelik, F. *Magic Demystified*, Oregon, Metamorphous Press, 1982

Morris, Desmond. *Manwatching*, London, Jonathan Cape, 1985

Malandro, L.A., Baker, L. & Barker, D. *Non-verbal Communication*, New York, Random House, 1989

Richmond, V.P., McCroskey, J. & Payne, S.K. *Non-verbal Behaviour in Interpersonal Relations*, New York, Prentice Hall, 1991

Knapp, M. & Hall, J. *Non-verbal Communication in Human Interaction*, Orlando, Holt, Rinehart and Winston, 1992

Grinder, John & Bandler, Richard. *The Structure of Magic II*, Palo Alto, Science & Behavior Books, 1976

BIBLIOGRAPHY

Bakan, P. 'The eyes have it', *Psychology Today*, 4 (1971), pp. 64–7, 96

Bakan, P. & Strayer, F. 'On reliability of conjugatelateral eye movements', *Perceptual and Motor Skills*, 36 (1973), pp. 429–30

Boulton, Michael & Smith, Peter. 'Rough and tumble play in children: Research and theory' *Infancia-y-apprendizaje*, 48 (1989), pp 79–91

Caparrotta, Luigi. 'Some thoughts about the function of gaze-avoidance in early infancy: A mother-baby observation', *Psychoanalytic-Psychotherapy*, 4(1) (1989), pp. 23–30

Ciabotti, Francesca & Maltempi, Antonio. 'Per una fenomenologia dell'espressione di "concentrazione" (Toward a phenomenology of the expression "concentration")', *Eta-evolutiva*, 12 (Jun. 1982), pp. 35–45

Cummings, E.; Vogel, Dena; Cummings, Jennifer &

El-Sheikh, Mona. 'Children's responses to different forms of expression of anger between adults', *Child Development*, 60(6) (Dec. 1989), pp. 1392–1404

Day, Trevor. *Positively Healthy*, Milton Keynes, The Chalkface Project, 1993

De-Long, Alton J. 'Yielding the floor: The kinaesthetic signals', *Journal of Communication*, 27(2) (Spring 1977), pp. 98–103

Elmore, C. Byron. 'Emotionally handicapped comprehension of non-verbal communication', *Journal of Holistic Medicine*, 7(2) (Fall-Winter 1985), pp. 194–201

Exline, R & Fehr B. 'Applications of Semiosis of the Study of Visual Interaction in Non-verbal Behavior and Communication', *Non-verbal Behavior and Communication*, (1978) pp. 117–57

Fisher & Byrne, D. 'Too close for comfort: Sex differences in response to invasions of personal space', *Journal of Personality and Social Psychology*, 32 (1975), pp. 15–21

Gamber, Paul. 'Roughhousing and fighting games among children from the perspective of comparative behavioural research: Implications for preschool and kindergarten education related to aggression and conflict', *Gruppendynamik*, 20(2) (May 1989), pp. 175–189

Gazzinga, M. *The Bisected Brain*, New York, Appleton Century and Croft, 1974

Ginsburg, Harvey; Pollman, Vicki & Wauson, Mitzi. 'An ethological analysis of non-verbal inhibitors of aggressive behavior in male elementary school children', *Developmental Psychology*, 13(4) (Jul. 1977), pp. 417–418

Hatch, Frank & Maietta, Lenny. 'The role of kinaesthesia in pre- and peri-natal bonding', *Pre- and Peri-natal Psychology*, 5(3) (Spring 1991), pp. 253–270

Henderson, Bruce. 'Describing parent-child interaction during exploration: Situation definitions and negotiations',

Genetic, Social and General Psychology Monographs, 117(1) (Feb. 1991), pp. 77–89

Hutt, C. & Ounstead, C. 'The biological significance of gaze aversion with particular reference to the syndrome of infantile autism', *Behavioural Science*, 11 (1966), pp. 346–56

Lang, Reuben & Frenzel, Roy. 'How sex offenders lure children', *Annals of Sex Research*, 1(2) (1988), pp. 303–317

Langlois, J.H. & Downs, A.C. 'Peer relations as a function of physical attractiveness: The eye of the beholder or behavioural reality?', *Child Development*, 50 (1970), pp. 409–418

Langlois, J.H.; Roggman, L.A.; Casey, R.J.; Ritter, J.M.; Rieser-Danner, L.A. & Jenkins, V.Y. 'Infant preferences for attractive faces: Rudiments of a stereotype?', *Developmental Psychology*, 23 (1987), pp. 363–9

Langlois, J.H. & Roggman, L.A. 'Attractive faces are only average', *Psychological Science*, 1 (1990), pp. 115–121

Lewis, Michael. 'Making Faces: Age and Emotion Differences in the Posing of Emotional Expressions', *Developmental Psychology*, 23 (1987), pp. 690–97

Madan-Swain, A. & Zentall, S.S. 'Behavioural comparisons of liked and disliked hyperactive children in play contexts and the behavioural accommodations by their classmates', *Journal of Consulting and Clinical Psychology*, 58(2) (Apr. 1990), pp. 197–209

Montemayor, Raymond & Flannery, Daniel. 'A naturalistic study of the involvement of children and adolescents with their mothers and friends: Developmental differences in expressive behaviour', *Journal of Adolescent Research*, 4(1) (Jan. 1989), pp. 3–14

Noller, Patricia & Callan, Victor. 'Non-verbal behaviour in families with adolescents',

Journal of Non-verbal Behaviour, 13(1) (Spring 1989), pp. 47–64

Nowicki, Stephen & Oxenford, Carolyn. 'The relation of hostile non-verbal communication styles to popularity in preadolescent children', *Journal of Genetic Psychology*, 150(1) (Mar. 1989), pp. 39–44

Phillips, Roger & Sellitto, Victoria. 'Preliminary evidence on emotions expressed by children during solitary play', *Play and Culture*, 3(2) (May 1990), pp. 79–90

Rotenberg, K.J. *Children's Interpersonal Trust*, Vienna, Springer Verlag, 1991

Saarni, Carolyn. 'Children's understanding of the interpersonal consequences of dissemblance of non-verbal emotional expressive behavior,' Special Issue: *Deception, Journal of Non-verbal Behaviour*, 12(4, part 2) (1988 Winter), pp. 275–294

Sheridan, Mary. 'Observations on the development of spontaneous tele-kinesic communication in babies and young children', *Childcare, Health & Development*, 3(3) (May–Jun. 1977), pp. 189–199

Trawick-Smith, J. 'Let's say you're the baby, OK? Play leadership and following behaviour of young children', *Young Children*, 43(5) (Jul. 1988), pp. 51–59

Woolfolk, A.E. 'Student learning and performance under varying conditions of teacher verbal and non-verbal evaluative communication', *Journal of Educational Psychology*, 70 (1987), pp. 87–94

INDEX

AUTHOR'S ACKNOWLEDGEMENTS

EDDISON·SADD

I should like to thank everyone who has helped me with this book. To begin with, I would like to thank the many families who helped me by filling in the questionnaire about children's body language. Most did so anonymously, but those who gave permission for me to mention them include: Alexander Babuta; Benedict Whynes and Jane Falk-Whynes; Benjamin, Daniel and June Bulley; Chloe; Consuelo Allen; Isobel Dacombe; Jane and Katy Hickman; Martin Brown; Ross Hubbard; S. Evans. Thank you in particular to Mrs Harban Kaur and the students from Harrow College of Further Education for making the questionnaire part of their nursery-placement project. And of course, special gratitude to John Seymour Associates and Joseph O'Connor, whose editorial mentions gained me many of my questionnaire respondents. My thanks too, to my agent Barbara Levy, and to Nick Eddison, Liz Eddison, Ian Jackson, Michele Turney, Marilyn Inglis, Hilary Krag and everyone at Eddison Sadd for their continuing help and support, and for making the writing of this book an enjoyable as well as a learning experience. Thanks also to Jennie Woodcock and all the children in the photographs. Dee McCullough, Susan Tarrant of the University of London Library and Caryl Hunter-Brown of the Open University Library at Milton Keynes were all helpful in my search for references and examples. My superb staff support team – June Bulley, Dot Gay and Felicity Sinclair – deserve both gratitude and praise for their continuing practical support. Finally, thank you to my husband Ian who, as always, makes all things possible.

Editorial Director Ian Jackson
Editors Michele Turney and Marilyn Inglis
Proofreader Tessa Rose
Indexer Dorothy Frame
Art Director Elaine Partington
Art Editor Hilary Krag
Picture Research Liz Eddison
Production Charles James and Hazel Kirkman

PICTURE CREDITS

t = top, b = below, l = left, r = right
All illustrations are credited to Reflections Photolibrary/Jennie Woodcock apart from the following:
Bubbles, page 21; Reflections/Jo Browne, page 22 1; Hutchison Library/ Anna Tully, pages 34–5; Bubbles/Loisjoy Thurston, page 37; Anthea Sieveking (with artwork overlay by Gordon Munro), pages 44–5; Bubbles/Loisjoy Thurston, page 46 tl; Bubbles, page 46 tr; Bubbles/Julie Fisher, page 46 bl; Bubbles/Jennie Woodcock, page 100; Bubbles/Claire Paxton, page 109; Bubbles/Loisjoy Thurston, page 113; Reflections/Colin Bowers, page 122.

Every effort has been made to trace photographers. Where acknowledgements are incomplete we apologize.